'The editors have produced an exceptional book that has relevance not only to graduate and beginning teachers, but also to those of us who have been teaching for many years. The chapters, written by outstanding science educators, provide inspiration and motivation to use research-based best practice to excite and engage our students in their studies of science for the 21st century.'

Stephen Zander, President, Australian Science Teachers Association

'This new edition brings much of the expert knowledge about science learning to secondary teachers in a very accessible and useful manner. The chapters on ICT and a "thinking" science classroom directly address two of the new challenges for teachers in the Australian Science Curriculum.'

Peter J. Fensham, Adjunct Professor of Science Education, QUT and Monash University

2nd edition

the art of TEACHING SCIENCE

For middle and secondary school

Edited by Grady Venville and Vaille Dawson

ALLEN&UNWIN
SYDNEY • MELBOURNE • AUCKLAND • LONDON

First published in Australia in 2012

Allen & Unwin
Sydney, Melbourne, Auckland, London

83 Alexander Street
Crows Nest NSW 2065
Australia
Phone: (61 2) 8425 0100
Fax: (61 2) 9906 2218
Email: info@allenandunwin.com
Web: www.allenandunwin.com

Cataloguing-in-Publication details are available from the
National Library of Australia
www.trove.nla.gov.au

ISBN 978 1 74237 659 2

Typeset in 11/13 pt Legacy Serif Book by Midland Typesetters, Australia
Printed and bound in Australia by Griffin Press

10 9 8 7 6 5 4 3

The paper in this book is FSC® certified.
FSC® promotes environmentally responsible, socially beneficial and economically viable management of the world's forests.

CONTENTS

FIGURES, TABLES AND SNAPSHOTS

FIGURES

TABLES

SNAPSHOTS

CONTRIBUTORS

Amelia Druhan is the Director of Science by Doing, a secondary-science initiative of the Australian Academy of Science. She has a variety of experience in the roles of science teacher and educator. She regularly presents at national and international conferences and has extensive experience in the production of digital resources that encourage professional learning and discussion among teachers.

Reinders Duit is Professor Emeritus of Physics Education at the Leibniz Institute for Science and Mathematics Education (IPN) in Kiel, the national institute for science education research in Germany. His research interests include the role of students' and teachers' conceptions of teaching and learning science with an emphasis on conceptual change perspectives.

Denis Goodrum is an Emeritus Professor at the University of Canberra. He is presently chair of the ACT Teacher Quality Institute and Executive Consultant for Science by Doing. During his career he has been responsible for many national projects, including preparing the shaping paper for the Australian Curriculum: Science.

Mark W. Hackling is Professor of Science and Technology Education at Edith Cowan University. Mark taught secondary science and has been involved in pre-service science teacher education for nearly 30 years. He is currently providing leadership to several national science education research projects.

Donna King is a lecturer in science education at the Queensland University of Technology in Brisbane. She previously taught secondary science for ten years before becoming a pre-service teacher educator. Donna's research interests include context-based science teaching, emotional learning in socio-scientific issues and eventful learning in pre-service teacher education.

Graham McMahon has been involved with science and computer education for 24 years. Currently, he is an educational developer for the Faculty of Science and Engineering at Curtin University, in which he helps academic staff to develop their e-learning programs. His interests include the development of cognition in technology-rich environments.

Catherine Milne is an Associate Professor at New York University. Her research interests include urban science education, the history of science and the development of multimedia and digital games for science, technology, engineering and mathematics (STEM) education. She is the author of *The Invention of Science* and co-editor-in-chief of the journal *Cultural Studies of Science Education.*

Mary Oliver works at the University of Western Australia. She is an experienced science teacher and lecturer both in Australia and overseas. Mary's research interests are in equity, giftedness, professional learning, cognitive acceleration and educational neuroscience.

David Palmer is an Associate Professor at the University of Newcastle. He is an experienced science teacher, and currently teaches science curriculum and methods to primary teacher education students. His research interest is motivation in science.

Léonie J. Rennie is a Professor in the Science and Mathematics Education Centre at Curtin University. Her current research interests concern inclusivity in science curricula, with a focus on learning science and technology in integrated and out-of-school contexts, and the promotion of scientific literacy.

David Treagust is Professor of Science Education at the Science and Mathematics Education Centre, Curtin University. His research interests are related to understanding students' ideas about science concepts, particularly how these ideas can be understood through conceptual change and used to enhance curricula and improve teachers' classroom practice.

Russell Tytler is Professor of Science Education at Deakin University. He has taught science at both the secondary and tertiary levels, and has been active in state and national curriculum innovation, and in science teacher education. His research interests include student learning and reasoning in science, and pedagogy and teacher learning.

ABOUT THE EDITORS

Vaille Dawson is Professor of Science Education at Curtin University. She has taught science at the primary, secondary and tertiary levels, and currently teaches at the postgraduate level. Her research interests include socio-scientific issues, argumentation and decision-making, integration of ICT in science and research in tertiary science settings.

Grady Venville is Winthrop Professor of Science Education at the University of Western Australia. She has been a teacher and educator in Australia, Japan and England. She teaches science curriculum and methods to pre-service science teachers, and her main research interests include conceptual change, curriculum integration and cognitive acceleration.

PREFACE

The timing of this second edition of *The Art of Teaching Science* coincides with the implementation of the Australian Curriculum. For the first time in Australia, high school teachers all over this vast country will be planning and implementing their science lessons based on the same nationwide document. As a consequence, we have reinvigorated the book, including completely new chapters directly related to the national documents on science curriculum, engaging students in science, ICT in the science classroom and developing a 'thinking' science classroom. The remainder of the chapters have been either completely rewritten and/or updated. As a result, the book is once again state-of-the-art!

The chapters of this book are written by leading science educators who have been involved deeply in school-based research, teaching and teacher education. These science educators have translated the latest research findings into recommendations for practice. The book is written in an Australian context for an audience of prospective science teachers (middle and secondary school), who will need to construct a unique combination of knowledge and skills to engage and excite students, and to foster their understanding of science.

Science teaching is a noble occupation that allows people to pursue their interests in science, and, at the same time work with young people in their formative years. Preparing to become a teacher is challenging and time-consuming, and we envisage that this book will provide teacher educators and pre-service teachers with an additional resource to augment their classroom activities. It is also a valuable resource to which beginning teachers can refer as they move through their first years of teaching service and also return for reflection as they become more experienced. While based on the findings of a large body of science education research, the book has deliberately been written in a style that is accessible, particularly for undergraduate and postgraduate students who are new to the art of teaching science.

The Art of Teaching Science is at the cutting edge and embraces the full spectrum of contemporary reforms in education while addressing the essential foundational knowledge and skills that student science teachers require. This book incorporates a comprehensive approach underpinned by the notion of scientific literacy. The chapters also reflect a student-centred approach to science teaching as advocated in reform curriculum documents throughout the world. Moreover, the book presents contemporary constructivist theory in an easy-to-understand and engaging way that enables student teachers to develop the background knowledge necessary to successfully teach science and to interpret the principles of the new Australian curriculum.

We have retained the title of the book, which was originally used in an attempt to capture the essence of 'good' science teaching. Science teaching is concerned with creativity, imagination and beauty; it involves risk-taking and should be thought-provoking. Teaching science is essentially a human endeavour and the selection of chapters within this book reflects the unique intersection between the art and the science of teaching.

This second edition of the book retains the three sections into which the first edition was divided. The first section, Understanding the Art of Teaching Science, provides a theoretical base for the remainder of the book. Thus readers will become aware of theoretical perspectives on what science is, constructivism, alternative conceptions, conceptual change theory and how recent research findings have influenced teaching and learning. The second section, Implementing the Art of Teaching Science, provides an overview of the fundamental aspects of effective science teaching such as teaching strategies, planning, inquiry, curriculum and assessment. The third section, Extending the Art of Teaching Science, takes students beyond the basics and enables them to engage with and explore the important issues that face science educators today. This section includes chapters on the problem of engaging students in science, the use of information communication technology (ICT), how to challenge students to learn to think about science in powerful ways, and creating an equitable science classroom.

As active science education researchers and teachers in tertiary science education programs, we feel we have encapsulated within the chapters of this book a diverse and inspiring combination of readings that will stimulate reflection, discussion and debate by a new generation of science teachers.

Grady Venville and Vaille Dawson

PART I
UNDERSTANDING THE ART OF TEACHING SCIENCE

CHAPTER ONE
WHAT IS SCIENCE?

Catherine Milne

OUTCOMES

By the end of this chapter you will be able to:

- Develop a rich understanding of the nature of science as a construct of human action
- Understand that theories and laws are creative constructions that are always limited by data and form the basis of scientific explanations
- Evaluate arguments about the structure of science as a discipline in education
- Start to develop a personal philosophy about the nature of science that will inform your practice as a teacher of science

INTRODUCTION

I have always been concerned by the lack of conversation in science education about the nature of science and how teachers make decisions about what counts as science. Combined with this is a concern about how teachers interpret claims of textbook authors or curriculum developers about what constitutes science. So here is a little test. Are the examples presented in Snapshot 1.1 *science*? How did you decide? Note down any questions that come to you as you read each snapshot.

SNAPSHOT 1.1: Examples of science

Which of these three examples would you locate in science?

Example 1

Kathryn Aurora Gray, a 10-year-old girl from New Brunswick in Canada, was in the news for having just discovered a supernova using software that allowed her to make time comparisons of a specific area of the night sky near Galaxy UGC3378, which is about 240 million light years away.

Example 2

The Yanyuwa and Garrwa people of the southwest Gulf of Carpentaria in Australia use cycads for food (Bradley, 2005). In the Yanyuwa language, the cycad is classified as *wurrana*, or 'being of authority', with economic and religious significance to the maritime environment. Use of the nut of the *wurrana*, also called cycad (*Cycas angulata*), as a food source constitutes a challenge because the nut, located inside the fruit, contains a neurotoxin. In order to remove the toxin, the Aborigines treated the nuts by heating them on hot stones or in ashes and then pounding or grinding them into flour. Grinding stones used to grind the nuts are often found in groves of cycad palms. The flour is strained using a tool made from fronds to leach out the toxin without losing the flour. From this flour, a bread called damper can be made.

The fruits of wurrana (*Cycas angulata*) used to make flour.

Example 3

In 1988, the science journal *Nature* published a paper (Davenas et al., 1988) of which the lead author was Jacques Benveniste, head of a biomedical laboratory run by the French National Institute of Health and Medical Research (INSERM). The research team was studying the antibody response in basophils, a type of white blood cell. They found that basophils showed an allergic response even when the antibody solutions used were so dilute that there was a 'calculated absence' of any antibody at the highest dilutions—basically, no antibodies were left in solution. Benveniste and his colleagues argued that since the effects were observed when the dilutions were accompanied by vigorous shaking, transfer of biological information was related to the molecular structure of water. One of the challenges for this area of study is that liquid water at the molecular level behaves in a way that is still not fully understood. The press called this phenomenon 'water memory'. Anyone familiar with homeopathy might see a relationship between this study and homeopathic remedies requiring high levels of dilution. In an unprecedented step, the editor of *Nature* at the time led a team of 'fraud busters' who demanded that the studies be repeated with external observers; when they were, the results were inconclusive.

Which of these examples would you locate within science? How would you make that decision? Do you focus on whether the case described was a study of nature? Do you focus on where the study was published? Do you focus on the procedures the researchers used to produce the knowledge? Do you focus on whether the data produced have been confirmed by others? Do you focus on whether a scientific theory was central to each case? Or is there some other aspect of each case that influences your decision about whether or not it belongs to science? Your response to each example is indicative of your understanding of what science is and its boundaries. You might also be asking: Well, what is the right answer? Which of these examples is really science? Unfortunately, the answers to those questions are not simple. Equally unfortunately, science textbooks often try to maintain the myth that there is a simplistic scientific method that, if followed, will allow you to say you are doing science. As these examples suggest, however, there are cultural and historical structures and accepted ways of doing things that are referred to as *associated norms*, which support people involved in the field of science when they need to decide what counts as science.

Importantly, I hope you will agree that each of these examples has some features that are important for identifying an endeavour as scientific. Each has something to say to us about the following statement: the practice of science involves humans called scientists working in a field of study with structures and values or norms that are used by members of the field of science to decide what should count as science. These structures and norms are developed by humans and applied to knowledge claims, and serve to define the field and boundaries of science. For example, the demand by the editor of *Nature* that Benveniste and his colleagues *replicate* their experiments with *witnesses* and generate similar data to those obtained in the study they submitted is an extreme example of some of the structures that the science community has in place to organise what counts as science. Other scientists were critical of the decision of the editor of *Nature* to publish this paper, suggesting a *communal* structure to decisions about what counts as science. As *Nature*'s editor acknowledged, the results were startling and seemed inconsistent with long-standing *scientific laws* such as the Law of Mass Action (a *mathematical model* of the constant relationship between the concentration of products and reactants in chemical reactions that reach dynamic equilibrium). He decided, therefore, that the investigation needed to be explored further rather than dismissed. All of the examples challenge us to ask whether there are structures or norms in place that provide some control of people who do science and who can be identified as *scientists*.

How did you respond to Example 2 involving Aboriginal groups from the Gulf of Carpentaria extracting flour from a toxic nut? This case raises the question of the role of *Indigenous knowledge* in the science students learn at school. As a form of systematic knowledge, how is Indigenous knowledge similar to, and different from, the science that typically informs curricula in the fields of science? I think of science (the science typically taught in schools) as a local knowledge that has gone global. Historically, the dispersion of the systematic knowledge we call *science* was helped by its association with languages, such as Greek, Latin and Arabic, which were the *lingua franca* of large swathes of Africa, Asia and Europe. What role does language play in Indigenous knowledge? Consider the role that English now plays in the communication of scientific knowledge. If all forms of systematic knowledge about the natural world are called science, then the science typically taught in schools might more accurately be called Eurocentric science, which indicates the place from which this form of science emerged over time.

What do curriculum documents say about science?

Often when science is offered as a subject at school, little thought is given to how we identify the borders of science that allow someone to make the claim that they are teaching or learning science. Instead, youth know they are doing science—or biology, or living environment, or physics, or whatever—based on the context of the school classroom in which this activity takes place or the resources—like textbooks—that they use.

If we look at the curriculum documents, we can get a sense of how specific groups of people frame their response to the question 'What is science?' For example, in Australia the Australian Curriculum, Assessment and Reporting Authority describes science in its publication The *Australian Curriculum: Science* (2012) as a dynamic, collaborative, forward-looking endeavour arising from human curiosity and a desire to make sense of our world through exploring, investigating and solving problems. Thoughtful scholars developed this working description using available resources and their experience in the field. Their goal is that teachers will use the description to develop curriculum. But how this proposal is enacted and enforced is a political and cultural decision. The social and cultural decisions that structure science focus on knowledge and how we come to know (*epistemology*), about what reality is (*ontology*), and about the values that are key to science (*axiology*). In the following sections, we will examine some of the epistemological elements of science beginning with *questions*.

THE NATURE AND ROLE OF QUESTIONS IN SCIENCE

Think back over the examples you read in Snapshot 1.1. Were there any questions you asked as you read each one? Did any of the questions you asked explore the science context further? For example, two questions that came to me after hearing about Kathryn Gray and her discovery of a supernova were: Are supernovas more likely to be observed in specific locations in the Universe or are they spread out equally all over the Universe? And how does one go about finding a supernova? (I do not have an issue with 10-year-olds making discoveries in science.) Note that the questions I asked—and perhaps the ones you asked too—make some assumptions about the world. For example, the way I asked my questions assumes that I can investigate them using logical means and that the phenomenon being explained will respond to inquiry in ways that are predictable. The belief that *nature behaves in predictable ways* is a cornerstone of science. In order to answer these questions, I do not expect to have to evoke anything else—such as supernatural beings or magic—for answers.

One way we can think about the discipline of science is as a series of questions, asked by people called scientists, about nature. Within a scientific framework, such questions allow us to gather information and solve problems. But if we think of scientists as questioning, then we also need to acknowledge that what we accept as the answer is partly determined by the question we ask. In other words, we are trying to make sense of the world, and we know some things that seem to fit together but there are also gaps, so we ask questions to fill in those gaps. Note that in science, in order to ask questions that will support further construction of science knowledge, you need to know something about that field first; you need to have some understanding of what the gaps are. For me, this is a key element in understanding how to support science inquiry in schools. Questions that can be explored do not come from nothing, so students need some background to ask questions that they can explore through the processes associated with science. Sources of this background can come from their everyday experiences. For example, the 2010–11 Queensland floods might lead students to ask whether the floods were due to climate change or just an example of a cyclical process. Observing the level of car traffic in downtown Sydney, students might ask whether the levels of ozone are worse there than near the site of a factory near their home. (Of course, in order to ask about ozone one would have to have some experience or knowledge of ozone.)

Within the cultural discipline of science, the types of questions asked are *what*, *how* and *why*. Into which of these types of questions can you fit the questions you asked as you read the examples in Snapshot 1.1? Different research methods are associated with each of these different types of question. For scientists—and perhaps also for students working in science—questions often come from unexpected results of experiments, results that do not conform to their expectations. There are lots of examples of this from the history of science, just like Snapshot 1.2, which tells a story about Marie and Pierre Curie discovering two new elements, polonium and radium. As you read through this example, think about what was known about this field before Marie Curie decided to become involved. Think of the question she decided to explore and how she made sense of the answer.

SNAPSHOT 1.2: A story about creating a new field of science: Radioactivity

Antoine Henri Becquerel, a French physicist, discovered Becquerel rays in January 1896 when he began to explore the question of whether all phosphorescent material emitted rays similar to x-rays discovered by Wilhelm Roentgen in November 1895. Becquerel decided to study uranium salts because he knew they gave off very strong phosphorescence and absorption spectra. Phosphorescence is an effect of substances that are able to absorb light energy and release it back over time. However, Becquerel discovered that the uranium salt did not need to be in sunlight to emit rays. He observed that the rays seemed to be emitted all the time. This behaviour was different from x-rays, which needed an energy source. Becquerel also noted that his rays seemed to have some effect on the electrical character of the surrounding environment.

Marie and Pierre Curie were intrigued by Becquerel's account of his discovery. Marie Curie wrote:

> Our attention was caught by a curious phenomenon discovered in 1896 by Henri Becquerel. The discovery of the x-ray by Roentgen had excited the imagination, and many physicians were trying to discover if similar rays were not emitted by fluorescent bodies under the action of light. With this question in mind Henri Becquerel was studying uranium salts, and, as sometimes occurs, came upon a phenomenon different from what he was looking for: the spontaneous emission by uranium salts of rays of a peculiar character . . . The study of this phenomenon seemed to us very attractive and all the more so because the question was entirely new and nothing yet had been written upon it. I decided to undertake an investigation of it. (Curie, 1929, pp. 93–4)

Marie Curie decided to examine other minerals and elements by modifying an instrument developed by Pierre Curie to measure the ionisation of the air exposed to the sample, and using that information to calculate the level of radiation. She expected to confirm Becquerel's earlier studies that the purer the sample of uranium, the more rays were released. However, when she compared high-quality pitchblende (uraninite) against pure uranium metal she found that the pitchblende was releasing more rays than the pure uranium. How could that be? As she records in her autobiographical notes, the pitchblende was four to five times more active than expected based on the amount of uranium present. She confirmed that her finding was not due to experimental error, so what was the cause? Marie suggested that there must be another more active material—perhaps a previously undiscovered element—existing with uranium in the mineral.

Note that Marie Curie's finding of higher radioactivity (a term she proposed) from pitchblende than from uranium metal was unexpected. Her first move was to check the instrument she used to detect the rays to make sure that what she had observed was not an artefact of instrument calibration but could be attributed to the material she was observing. Once she had established that the instrumentation was reliable and accurate, she had to find another possible explanation for what was causing this ray activity. She addressed this question by looking for a new element using spectra, an innovative method initially developed by Robert Bunsen and Gustav Kirchhoff. Bunsen and Kirchhoff discovered caesium and rubidium using spectra in 1860 and 1861 respectively (each element has a unique spectrum, so a sample of a new element would be expected to emit a unique spectrum). Her explanation/hypothesis was that extra ray activity was due to a previously unidentified element or two present in pitchblende, and once she had reached a certain level of purity, she used spectra to look for these new elements.

Let us compare Marie Curie's approach to addressing a question of interest to her with the activities of a group of students in Snapshot 1.3.

SNAPSHOT 1.3: How to frame a question for investigation

A biology teacher decided to adopt an inquiry-based biology curriculum. The students in the course were excited by the idea that they would be doing research in their biology class. They began by discussing with the teacher the questions they could investigate. Understandably, the students' access to rats, mice and guinea pigs—they were living in the classroom—had some influence on the students' choice of question. They had observed these animals over a number of weeks and were interested in providing other environments in which to observe them completing various tasks. The students decided to investigate the question: Which are more intelligent, rats, mice or guinea pigs? Is this question refined enough to allow students to conduct a scientifically based inquiry? If you were the teacher, what would you do to support students to explore some aspect of this question?

Here are some general suggestions—by no means exhaustive—that might help these students to refine their question and also might help any group of students refine a question they have about phenomena while concurrently suggesting subsequent investigations. How do these ideas compare with your thinking?

- What purpose is served by this question (in other words, why would anybody be interested in finding an answer to this question)? In the case of the rodents, you might have asked the students why anyone would be interested in the comparative intelligence of guinea pigs, rats and mice. This means you need to have a rationale for the inquiry. A question of this nature introduces students to the cultural and social dimensions of question asking. When conducting scientific inquiry, scientists support the relevance of their question by providing a review of current research and arguing that their research will build on the scientific knowledge that currently exists, like Marie Curie did.
- What can you find out about rodent (animal) intelligence that has already been published? This question reinforces the twin ideas that your investigation is located within a broader area of research and that you should use the research outcomes or knowledge that already exists to inform your own study or studies. This step also reminds you that both knowledge and ignorance are necessary for inquiry. Sometimes this can be forgotten in classroom settings, but

helping students to recognise what they do and do not know about the phenomenon they wish to study will help them to understand the value of searching to find out what is already known about similar phenomena and how they could use this information to inform their own research. At this stage, students might also be encouraged to carry out some simple observations of the organism or phenomenon, and think about instruments they might need to help them develop the data they need to answer the questions they wish to investigate. This might help them to structure their ongoing questions and resolve some of their ignorance about the phenomenon they wish to study.

- How will you define/operationalise 'intelligence' for this study? You need to decide how to define and model a term such as 'intelligence'. This question might emerge in the planning of the inquiry as students develop instruments to test the intelligence of various animals. In the case described, the students wanted to build mazes to test the intelligence of these rodents, and in the process of developing their mazes also began to examine questions related to the challenges of developing useful instruments and how their instrumentation could affect the observations they could make. This might lead you to an examination of the question of how definitions and models can affect the design of investigations.

As the case of the students exploring rodent intelligence indicates, only some questions can be explored using tools that are culturally and socially associated with science. Science also is a balancing act because typically when you ask a question, you anticipate the answer, so there is challenge associated with not letting anticipation lead you to make claims that you cannot support with evidence. In other words, try not to be seduced by what you think the answer should be.

OBSERVATIONS AND THE NATURE OF A FACT

Reflect back on Marie Curie's experience in Snapshot 1.2 and think about how that experience compares with the way science is typically taught in science classrooms. As Curie explored the rays released by various substances, she had to verify that the observations of the phenomena she was presenting were truthful—that is, that they had the character of a fact. We can understand an *observation* as using our senses, or instruments that extend our senses, to make statements about what seems real. For example, you walk outside on a summer's day. Applying your sense of touch, you feel hot. This is an observation. We can think of a scientific fact as an idea developed by scientists, or a *construction*. A scientific fact is based on an observation that has been confirmed through processes of multiple cases and multiple witnesses and, sitting in the background often unacknowledged, is a theory that gives significance to the facts that are being constructed. In Marie Curie's case, what counted as a fact was based on both the phenomenon that she was observing and personal and public theories associated with understanding these rays. If she had no knowledge of this area of science, she would not have thought to ask questions about rays and she would not have thought to record the level of radiation.

Facts are constructed from observations, which can be thought of as systematic perceptions—that is, how we use our senses to understand the natural world. My experience of teaching a Year 8 unit on cells emphasised for me the role of theory in observing. I had taught a four-week unit that involved students in observing many different cell types and cell structures. I was feeling pretty proud of myself. The students seemed to be enjoying themselves and seemed very actively engaged in the activities. Towards the end of the unit, I asked one of the students whether he was getting good cells from his sample. 'Yes, Miss,' he replied. 'I can see lots of round cells with dark walls.' I realised right away, much to my dismay, that he was describing air bubbles, not cells! How difficult it is to 'see' cells was well captured by Robert Hooke in his famous book, *Micrographia* (2003 [1665]), where he writes about what he observed when he began to use his new tool, the microscope. He struggled to describe to his readers what he saw when he looked down his microscope at a small sample of cork. He used metaphor, describing the shapes he observed as 'perforated and porous much like a honeycomb' and saying that 'these pores or cells were not very deep'. He was, of course, describing what came to be called *cells*. Often in the telling of this story in science textbooks, however, Hooke's struggles are not presented. Wouldn't it be better for learners if they were?

This experience was an 'ah ha' moment for me, bringing together a number of previous experiences, and leaving me with an awareness, which I applied to my teaching practice, that unless a student has some knowledge of what something is like (a personal theory), then the student's chance of observing that phenomenon is much reduced.

From that and other experiences, I took away the understanding that observations cannot be theory free. Your observation of any phenomenon is shaped by your experience of that phenomenon. The experience of scientists allows them to observe phenomena as specialists rather than as novices. In a way, this is part of the mission of science educators: to support students to 'see' the world in ways with which they have had little previous experience.

UNDERSTANDING AND EXPLANATION

Within the culture of science, there is an expectation that if another researcher wants to replicate an inquiry—such as Curie's study—and obtain the same results, they should be able to do so. Remember from Snapshot 1.1 the challenges Benveniste and his colleagues faced in trying to replicate their results for water memory. If you think about the way science is often taught in schools, scientific phenomena are presented to students not as observations open to interpretation, but as secure and true facts. One consequence of this approach is that the scientific explanations are based on information that, for students, is not debated or available to be contested. This means that often the laboratory work students do is based on verifying, or reproducing, information that supports facts which are already known. For example, as a teacher you might have a teaching and learning objective or statement: *Students understand that the Earth is composed of materials that are altered by forces within the Earth and on its surface.* The idea of *understanding* and the idea of *explanation* are interdependent. In order *to explain* you need *to understand*, and in order to show you understand, you need to be able to explain. Note also that in this learning statement the phenomenon, *the Earth is composed of materials that are altered by forces within the Earth and on its surface*, is accepted as permanently true, so understanding in this case is based on phenomena that are not open to question. What seems to be missing from this learning statement is any consideration of a way to explain how and why these Earth forces are present. For me, the search for *mechanisms*—usually presented in scientific theories—to explain why specific phenomena or facts can be constructed is a fundamental element of the field of Eurocentric science.

An understanding of the role of mechanisms should be a focus of science taught in schools. Mechanisms can be described as fundamental processes associated with—perhaps even responsible for—natural phenomena. The idea of a mechanism is central to the development of scientific explanations and is associated with cause-and-effect reasoning, which accepts that events are connected as cause and effect. Mechanisms also have their limitations because they are associated with the idea that we can understand natural processes because they are like machines. Although this model of the Earth as a machine has been very productive for science, it is still a model and can limit our understanding of the world if it is the only model used.

Explanations are central to answers. Once you get an answer to your question, you are left to decide how you can make the claim that Answer A is a real answer to Question 1. Typically, in science, it is considered important to not only generate observations associated with a specific question, but also to associate these observations with a pre-existing theory or model that helps us to *explain* why those observations were made and how they answer the question appropriately. To explain is not to answer a question, but to supply the missing extra information that makes the conditions for a convincing answer to a question. In general, a scientific explanation is composed of an observation or observations that are used as evidence; it warrants, usually, theories, models or laws that support the use of these observations to make this explanation. This is what constitutes a *scientific world-view*, a culturally dependent belief that explanations exist to help us better understand and explain the natural world. You might notice some similarities here between what I have labelled an explanation and what you might think of as an argument. In my view, an explanation and an argument in science share characteristics, but I think the emphasis for each is somewhat different. In an explanation the emphasis is on *making data comprehensible* with *reference to a specific accepted model/theory*. In an argument, the focus is on *using evidence from data/observations/facts* to *make a claim* that is *warranted by a specific model/theory*.

DATA, FACTS, PATTERNS AND LAWS

Data become facts when they are associated with a specific theory or model. Typically, science seeks to organise data into patterns with the expectation that such order is part of nature, and by revealing these patterns science is providing humans with greater insight into how the Earth and the Universe work. Can you think how science is able to do this? Read through Snapshot 1.4 and answer the question before reading on.

SNAPSHOT 1.4: Looking for patterns

Archaeopteryx is an extinct animal that possesses both scales and feathers, and at one stage was thought to be the 'missing link' between lizards and birds. Only six fossil specimens exist and they vary greatly in size. As a result, there has been a lot of discussion about whether the fossils all belong to one species or to different species. In order to help answer this question, data from the length (cm) of the femur (a leg bone) was plotted against the length of the humerus (a bone in the arm) on a scatter plot (see figure). These data were available for five of the specimens. If the specimens belong to the same species and the differences are due to differences in size because of age, then the points should show a linear positive relationship. If all the fossils belong to different species, then there should be no association and if one of the specimens belongs to a different species from the others then you should be able to observe an outlier.

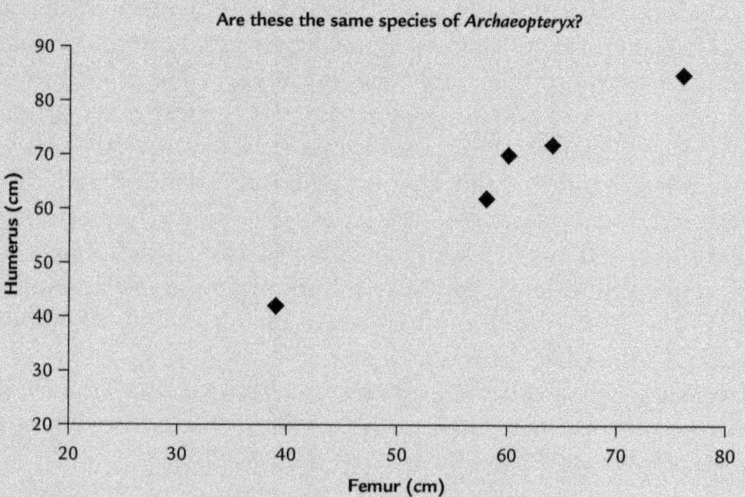

What does the scatter plot indicate?

(a) No association indicates that five separate species are present.
(b) An outlier can be observed, indicating the presence of two separate species.
(c) There is a strong positive association, indicating that the specimens belong to one species.
(d) It is not possible to make any statement about the possible number of species present from the data provided.

Did you select (c) as your answer? Well done! The researchers also produced scatter plots of the length of other bones such as the ulna, tibia and teeth against femur length and obtained similar relationships. These results led them to conclude that the fossils were consistent with a single species of different sizes, none of which was fully grown. In order to have a sense of how robust this apparent relationship might be, what other questions would you think to ask?

Another strategy for making facts more compelling is to look for patterns in the facts that can be represented as a scientific *law*. Finding patterns in data is a creative act. If these patterns are found in other places and at other times, and it seems that the patterns are consistent through time and space, then other scientists are more likely to accept that the patterns described exist in nature. The identification of a pattern is an initial criterion needed for the formulation of laws from observations of phenomena. Intuition and creativity is needed for someone to make a claim for a relationship or pattern in data that can be framed as a law. For me, this creativity is one aspect of science that is neglected in typical representations of laws in science education. A law represents a statement, often mathematical, describing a phenomenon that does not vary through space or time. A simple example is Boyle's Law. The discovery of this law was associated with a number of experimental philosophers in seventeenth century Europe, but in 1662 Robert Boyle achieved notoriety by publishing a paper outlining the law. The phenomenon Boyle explored was the relationship between gas pressure and volume. Boyle wrote about this law before decimals and coordinate geometry (used to show relationships between variables) were generally accepted. The relationship can be represented mathematically as:

$pV = k$ *(constant) at constant temperature.*

When presented in the form $P_1V_1 = P_2V_2$, this law can be used to make predictions. Physicist Richard Feynman (1964) recognised the constructed and creative nature of scientific laws in his comment, 'Nature obeys an elegant law. How clever she is to pay attention to it.' The power of laws lies in their utility. They allow scientists to make predictions. Feynman claimed that laws were simple and beautiful in pattern, but not in action. By this he meant that a law could look simple, be represented by a simple mathematical formula, but have implications far beyond the specific context in which it initially was proposed.

SCIENTIFIC LAWS AND THEORIES

Boyle's Law works under most conditions that we experience, but not at extremes of pressure and temperature. Boyle proposed this law based on observations of the effect of mercury on the volume of air trapped at the end of the mercury in a glass tube, which he was able to support by showing how the observations were consistent with his prediction of an inverse relationship between pressure and volume. The law can also be derived theoretically from the motion of particles, which Daniel Bernoulli did in his book *Hydrodynamica* in 1738–although his work was virtually ignored at the time because his scientific colleagues had other questions they found more compelling. Even Robert Boyle used the particle theory, by using the term 'corpuscles' to explain his observations about air. He argued that the concept of particles in motion could be used to explain many natural phenomena observed by experimental and natural philosophers. The corpuscular theory of matter was part of the experimental conversation in the seventeenth century, so it is understandable that Boyle creatively applied his understanding of the theory, a conceptual framework, to explain the behaviour of the air he observed (I make him sound very modern, but by the eighteenth century, theories like the caloric theory of heat provided far more powerful explanatory frameworks and were in use until the middle of the nineteenth century).

So scientific laws exist between facts and theories and we can come at them from either direction. Typically, however, they are associated with data, and if data do not support a law in its current form, then the law can be tweaked to accommodate new data. It takes creativity to infer a law from observed phenomena and it takes more creativity to propose a theoretical explanation for the phenomena and the patterns constructed from observations of phenomena. I think of scientific theories, and their associated models, as the explanatory frameworks for science, providing the needed mechanisms to explain phenomena. In particular, I have in mind theories like atomic theory, kinetic molecular theory, evolution, plate tectonics, cell theory and special relativity. All theories in science have the potential to be transformative because they support scientists to ask different questions. A case in point is plate tectonics, which is the focus of Snapshot 1.5.

SNAPSHOT 1.5: Theorising plate tectonics

If you studied geology in the 1950s or early 1960s you would have had to learn the geology of specific regions of Australia or the Indian and Pacific Oceans because each region was thought to be different. At that time, there was no unifying theoretical basis for understanding the Earth's geology. But the theory of plate tectonics changed all that. Plate tectonics explains large motions of the Earth's crust and upper mantle based on the idea that the Earth's surface is broken into tectonic (built) plates that float on the upper mantle.

The theory of continental drift, proposed by Alfred Wegener in 1912, was known but there was no compelling evidence that could be used with this theory to explain how continents drifted. Fossil evidence, such as the discovery of fossil seed ferns, *Glossopteris*, over South Africa and India, had been used to support the argument for continental drift but the geological community in the early twentieth century did not consider that the evidence was compelling enough to support this theory. In the first half of the twentieth century, the accepted model of the Earth's interior was that it consisted of a liquid core and a solid mantle, and such a model made it difficult to explain how continents could drift when the mantle was solid. Applying geologic and tectonic observations, in 1954 S. Warren Carey (1911–2002), an Australian geologist and advocate of continental drift, proposed an expanding Earth hypothesis to provide a mechanism to explain how continents could drift to form the continental organisation we observe today (he had earlier proposed subduction as the driving mechanism but was unable to get his paper published). The discovery in the upper mantle of metamorphic rocks (serpentinised peridotite), formed from low pressure and temperature, supported American Harry Hess's argument that convection in the Earth's mantle was the driving force behind island arcs, like Hawaii, and the explanation for a phenomenon he called sea floor spreading. The geological community found the evidence for subduction and sea floor spreading more compelling than the evidence presented for the expanding Earth hypothesis. The ability to measure the age of the ocean floor confirmed a prediction made by the sea floor spreading hypothesis, and did not require an expanding Earth. Carey continued to be a supporter of the expanding Earth hypothesis, but he was definitely in the minority.

There is no doubt that the theory of plate tectonics has transformed understanding of the geology and paleoecology of the Earth. In this example of a scientific theory and its mechanisms, we focused on plate tectonics and I would like you to think about some other important scientific theories and the mechanisms that are core elements of those theories. Consider evolution. What is a mechanism that is part of evolution? Consider kinetic molecular theory. What is a mechanism for that theory? The disciplinary power of scientific theories and their internal mechanisms is that they have both explanatory and predictive power.

What is interesting to me is how over time these theories evolve from local knowledge to general, and in science's case become a form of global knowledge. Scientific inquiry is a kind of purposeful and directed curiosity that brings together questions, data and theory to generate arguments or explanations. What can science tell us? How is science limited? Typically, you might argue that science can only explore knowledge that is available for investigation and associated with the natural physical world. You might also argue that science can only tell us about the Universe *as it is* not the Universe *as it ought to be.* Such an argument might then lead us to accept that while science can help us understand the world, it cannot tell us how we ought to lead our lives in that world. Such an argument also challenges us because some people might use it to argue that there is no place for values in science; however, as we have seen, there are some values that are absolutely central to the practice of science. For example, science made it okay to be curious, found a place for quantification, accepts that nature is real and knowable, and follows rules that can be discovered. How science makes sense of the world through the use of questions, facts, laws, hypotheses and theories is a strategy that can be used to distinguish between understandings and beliefs that are accepted as scientific, and understandings and beliefs that exist outside of science, but we also should acknowledge that it is only one form of systematic knowledge and not the only form.

SUMMARY OF KEY POINTS

Science is a global form of systematic knowledge. Central to science is a specific way of asking questions that assumes we can attain answers to those questions by using our senses to observe the world naturally or through experiments in which we change the world in some way. This approach is based on our belief that nature behaves in predictable ways. Science is also based on the idea that in these observations we can find patterns that tell us more about the organisation of nature. For example, Boyle was able to claim an inverse relationship between pressure and volume in a gas. This relationship has been supported by experiments conducted in other places and times (you might even have carried out an experiment to confirm this relationship), so it has become a law. But even though laws allow us to make predictions, as Boyle was able to do, they do not help us to understand why this relationship can be observed. For that we need a theory.

Science is also a field of endeavour constructed by humans, and in the end it is the science community that decides what counts as science. It is the community that judges whether claims for new knowledge, such as those presented in the snapshots involving Kathryn Gray, Jacques Benveniste and Marie Curie, are convincing. In summary, Eurocentric science—the science represented in science classrooms all over the globe—is one community's attempt to explain the world in ways that influence every living thing on this planet. As an educator, your goal should be to engage your students in a science that captures aspects of the communal and knowledge processes that are involved.

DISCUSSION QUESTIONS

1.1 What is scientific about the practices of the Yanyuwa and Garrwa people described in Snapshot 1.1?

1.2 Using the example of Boyle's Law, draw a mind map or concept map showing the relationships between patterns, observations, theory and law.

1.3 Using the material presented in this chapter, explain why evolution or kinetic molecular theory is a scientific theory.

1.4 How has your reading of this chapter informed your thinking about your teaching practice in science?

REFERENCES

Australian Curriculum, Assessment and Reporting Authority (2012). *The Australian Curriculum: Science*. Canberra: Commonwealth of Australia.

Bradley, J. J. (2005). 'Same time poison, same time good tucker': The cycad palm in the south west gulf of Carpentaria. *Journal of Australian Studies*, *29*, 119–133.

Curie, M. (1929). *Pierre Curie*. C. & V. Kellog (trans.). New York: Macmillan.

Davenas, E., Beauvias, F., Amara, J., Oberbaum, M., Robinzon, B., Miadonna, A., Tedeschi, A., Pomeranz, B., Fortner, P., Belon, P., Sainte-Laudy, J., Poitevin, B., & Benveniste, J. (1988). Human basophil degranulation triggered by very dilute antiserum against IgE. *Nature, 333,* 816–818.

Feynman, R. (1964). *The character of physical law*. BBC video. Retrieved 20 November 2011 from http://research.microsoft.com/apps/tools/tuva/#data=3.

Hooke, R. (2003 [1665]). *Micrographia*. Mineola, NY: Dover.

Houck, M. A., Gauthier, J. A., Strauss, R. E. (1990). Allometric scaling in the earliest fossil bird, *Archaeopteryx lithographica*. *Science, 247,* 195–198.

Vine, F. J., & Matthews, D. H. (1963). Magnetic anomalies over oceanic ridges. *Nature, 199,* 947–949.

CHAPTER TWO

CONSTRUCTIVIST AND SOCIO-CULTURAL VIEWS OF TEACHING AND LEARNING

Russell Tytler

OUTCOMES

By the end of this chapter you will be able to:

- Describe and give examples of students' existing conceptions in science
- Distinguish between different views of learning, including constructivist and socio-cultural perspectives
- Describe what learning might involve from these different perspectives

INTRODUCTION

This chapter looks at the implications of a substantial body of research that has changed the way we think about learning and understanding in science. Many of the findings about student conceptions are surprising and intriguing, and now well established. There is considerable debate, however, about how we should best think about what students understand, and on what we should focus to support learning. Should we think of our task as finding challenges to change what is in individual students' heads, should we be primarily concerned with setting up rich and productive ways of talking and interacting in classrooms, or should we think of our task as inducting students into the literacy practices of the scientific community?

STUDENT CONCEPTIONS IN SCIENCE

It is by no means easy for students to come to grips with significant scientific concepts such as energy, adaptation or chemical change. Any teacher will have experienced the frustration of explaining a concept in what they thought was the clearest possible way, only to be faced with expressions of mute incomprehension (or worse). They will also have experienced interesting and seemingly productive conversations in class, only to find on testing that nothing much seems to have been gained at all. How can learning scientific concepts be so difficult? How can we do it better?

There is now an enormous body of research on student learning in science that focuses on the ideas students bring with them to the classroom, and the effect of these on how and what they learn. This research has stemmed from the realisation that children can emerge from a science unit with very different understandings from those intended by the teacher. Even where students perform at a high level on classroom tests, it has been found that they may display a range of very different understandings when asked to apply these ideas to other problems and contexts, especially out-of-school contexts. The main findings of this body of research can be summarised thus:

- Students come into our classes with a range of existing ideas or conceptions of the physical world. Their brains are not 'empty vessels' waiting to be filled with information.
- Many of these conceptions differ in important ways from the view of the world scientists have constructed (interestingly, many of these 'alternative'—or 'naïve'—conceptions are similar to views scientists held in previous eras).
- Students from different countries and cultures have been found to have very similar ideas, so that there seems to be a common set of alternative conceptions that are encouraged by untutored life experience and everyday language.

- These conceptions in many cases form useful prior knowledge on which a teacher can build. In many cases, however, students' alternative conceptions have proved surprisingly difficult to shift, and can offer a serious barrier to effective learning.

A large number of alternative conceptions that interfere with learning have been identified across a range of science topics. Examples of these alternative conceptions are described in the following paragraphs.

The first example is that students and many adults hold theories of motion similar to earlier impetus theories, where force is thought to be a property of an object associated with motion, rather than something that acts on an object externally to influence motion. Thus, when asked whether there is a force on a golf ball flying through the air, an adult may answer: 'Well, as it's still going forward, I would have thought yes, the force of the hit is still with it. If there were no force it would drop straight down.' This idea is incorrect from a scientific point of view (can you say why?) but it is quite understandable that many adults and children hold this view.

Another example of a common alternative conception is that young children interpret animal behaviour in terms of the animal's wishes (a psychological view), and find it difficult to think of behaviour as having an adaptive function. Thus a Year 3/4 child may say, in response to an observation that worms congregate in moist soil when given a choice: 'Because they might be dry and they wanted to be wet.' When asked why Himalayan rabbits' fur turns white in winter, they may say: 'They want to turn white. The white fur is stronger so he will be warmer' or 'So they can be different from other rabbits.' When asked about the effects of introducing European carp into Australian waterways, it has been observed that Year 3/4 children tend to think in terms of direct effects such as predation or muddying the water, whereas Year 5/6 children are more likely to talk about the second-order interactive effect of competition for food. Similarly, in response to the question 'Why do plants have flowers?' the main responses selected by 7 and 8-year-olds is 'to make them look nice' or 'because bees need the pollen and nectar', whereas older children look for explanations involving adaptation.

In chemistry, students are often influenced by an 'historical view' of substances in chemical change—thinking, for instance, that the ash left over from burning paper is simply the paper but in a changed form, or is something that was trapped in the paper and is now the residue, or that rust is simply iron in a different, broken-down form.

There are a number of alternative conceptions arising from the perceptual difficulties associated with air. For instance, children will be amazed that a tissue in an upturned glass remains dry when plunged into water. Older children and many, if not most, adults will explain the operation of a bird feeder (or the rubber 'suction' cap on a toy dart) in terms of 'suction' from the trapped air rather than differences in air pressure. This perceptual issue also underlies the difficulty students have with explaining the condensation that forms on the outside of cold objects such as a bottle of lemonade taken from the fridge (they often think the lemonade has seeped out), because such an explanation involves a conception of air containing water in gaseous form.

A final example of an alternative conception is that students often believe that heat is a substance rather than a form of energy. This results in them running the concepts of temperature and heat together—thinking, for example, that if a hot cup of coffee is divided the temperature is halved. These views also echo historical theories. A challenge you might take up for yourself is predicting what will be the outcome if thermometers are inserted inside a woollen glove, a cotton cloth, aluminium foil and damp paper compared with two uncovered thermometers, one of which rests on a metal surface, all left in the same room for a period of time. Will there be a difference in temperature?

Significant alternative conceptions often centre on concepts for which the common and scientific use of language differs—for example, 'animal' (Bell, 1993), 'energy', 'force', 'heat' or 'alive'. This helps explain why such conceptions can be extremely difficult to shift. Many studies have shown that they can persist despite carefully planned traditional teaching, and often despite students being able to gain high scores on science tests. Alternative conceptions thus have the capacity to interfere with learning in science if they are not acknowledged in planning teaching sequences.

When a student is presented with a scientific idea that differs from previously held conceptions, they may accept it or reject it totally, or accept it for the science class but continue to use their prior conceptions in their daily lives; sometimes they will form a hybrid conception combining the two.

HOW SHOULD WE VIEW THESE CONCEPTIONS?

There has been ongoing debate concerning the nature and status of these conceptions. Are they fledgling theories, coherent belief systems, mistakes of fact or judgement, or useful entry points into more powerful scientific conceptions? There are many terms used by researchers in this area that reflect these different views, including misconceptions (i.e. mistaken beliefs), alternative conceptions (i.e. different but valid ways of looking at the world), intuitive ideas (i.e. unformed) or interpretive frameworks (i.e. useful ways of making sense of the world). The term 'misconception', which tends now to be out of favour, implies that ideas students have are simply wrong when judged against 'correct' scientific conceptions. The implication of this is that we need to develop teaching strategies to circumvent their development, or to root them out when they are discovered. Such an interpretation devalues the very real conceptual content of some of these ideas, and discourages the development of new teaching approaches advocated by more thoughtful science educators, some of which are described in Chapters 3 and 4.

The term 'children's science', popular in the 1980s and 1990s, promoted a view of students constructing, from their everyday experience, conceptions that have some of the characteristics of scientific theories (a certain degree of self-consistency, logic and explanatory power, for instance) but are perhaps limited in scope of application and capable of misleading children in explaining a variety of phenomena. A similar emphasis is implied by the term 'alternative frameworks'. If this is the case, then the task of science teachers is to find ways of providing pathways to support students to undergo major shifts, or 'conceptual changes', in their perspectives, through recognising the greater power of the scientific way of looking at the world.

This 'conceptual change' idea received a lot of support from researchers throughout the 1980s and 1990s. The idea is appealing partly because of the often-quoted correspondence between children's ideas and those of earlier scientists, and the emergence of a view that major scientific advances involve revolutionary 'paradigm shifts' (Kuhn, 1970). Thus the change from an Earth-centred to a Sun-centred solar system and the emergence of a continental drift theory are regarded as 'revolutions' involving quite new ways of looking at the world. Researchers have drawn explicit parallels between the ideas of scientific revolutions and conceptual change in students, but is this really the case? And if so, over what time period might the change occur? Carey (1985) argues that children move slowly from a 'psychological' theory to a 'biological' theory of animal behaviour as they are exposed to an increasing amount of content knowledge and language. Over this time period, the way they view animals and the questions they ask change fundamentally as one would expect for a major theory change. There is argument, however, as to whether all learning is of this nature.

Why should this issue matter for us as teachers? If we consider that teaching these concepts is a process of fundamental theory change, then it helps to explain why learning about animal behaviour or Newtonian physics is so difficult. We are managers of personal scientific revolutions in the heads of our students! The argument is that we can't consider teaching as simply the clear explanation and demonstration of new ideas, but need to recognise these student views and be strategic in challenging them. On the other hand, in the animal behaviour case, we may take the view that teaching children about adaptive function is a long-term process that involves gradually chipping away at their naïve views and not being disheartened by incomplete adoption of the biological view.

Should we view these ideas as unhelpful childish perceptions to be eradicated? A number of writers have argued that anthropomorphic thinking (the view that animals and plants make decisions like humans) and teleological reasoning (the idea that there is a 'grand plan' guiding the way organisms behave)—both non-scientific perspectives—can be useful as platforms from which more sophisticated ideas can spring, and which may persist to support the scientific view. Other writers have questioned whether students really are consistent in the way they use either alternative or scientific ideas. Further, there is evidence to suggest that students do not abandon their intuitive conceptions once they learn to operate with a scientific conception, but carry them alongside, to be used in situations where the scientific conception is difficult to apply. They can even use a number of conceptions together, to provide different perspectives on the same event. For instance, in explaining why a glass full of water, when upturned with a card across the rim, does not empty, Gerry generates a series of ideas in discussion: 'it [the card] sticks to the glass'; 'it's holding it in with the air sort of stuck to it'; 'the air's suctioning up . . . sort of '; 'there's water and there's air and so the air must be making a cushion between them both'; 'Water and a tiny bit of air. Water and the air sort of trapping . . . water and the plastic are sort of trapping the air when it has water there'; 'no water and the air can just press it down'; 'yeah' ('it's like a plunger') (Tytler, 1998). Even adult scientists will carry a range of views about animals or energy or 'suction' alongside their more sophisticated understandings. Recently, there has been acceptance of the view that understanding and learning are richer and more complex than the

simple conceptual change model implies. Thus, as teachers, we should recognise the richness and variability of students' ideas, and find ways to both challenge and make use of them.

CONSTRUCTIVIST/CONCEPTUAL CHANGE PERSPECTIVES

The research into children's conceptions has raised questions about the nature of student learning, and indeed about the nature of knowledge—in particular, the status of scientific knowledge compared with students' intuitive conceptions. From the start, researchers recognised that learning should not be seen as some sort of conceptual implanting process or 'filling up' process (the 'jug and the empty mug' metaphor!), but that it involves an interplay between students' existing ideas and the knowledge or experiences to which they are exposed in the classroom. From this perspective, learning is viewed as the construction of personal meaning, and learning in the classroom is simply an extension of the same process by which the existing ideas were developed from students' active engagement and meaning-making with the world, from the earliest age. This individual, conceptual view of learning owes much to the child development theories of Jean Piaget (a Swiss developmental psychologist, 1896–1980), who viewed learning as arising from children's acting on the world. During the late 1980s and 1990s, these views were gathered under the more general label of 'constructivism' or a 'constructivist theory of knowledge'.

The points below represent a summary of this personal constructivist view of learning as it has been understood in the science education context. They are adapted from a 1980s document produced by the influential Children's Learning in Science group, based in Britain. Notice that while this view refers to the importance of language (a social phenomenon) in the construction of meaning, the emphasis is very much on the construction of conceptual meaning by individuals. It is very much a 'head' view of learning and knowledge, and lies firmly in the Piagetian tradition of focusing on the development of the individual mind.

A personal constructivist view of learning emphasises the following:

- Learning outcomes depend not only on the learning environment but also on the knowledge of the learner. The knowledge of the learner can assist or interfere with learning.

- Learning involves the construction of meaning. Meanings constructed by students from what they see or hear may be different from those intended, and are influenced by existing knowledge.
- The construction of meaning is a continuous and active process. Children struggle to construct meaning about their world from the time they are born, and this process continues both inside and out of school throughout their lives.
- There are identifiable patterns in the types of understandings students construct, due to shared experiences with the world and to cultural influences through language.
- Knowledge promoted in the science classroom is evaluated, and may be completely accepted, accepted in a limited way or rejected by the learner.
- Learners have the final responsibility for their own learning. Thus, a teacher can never learn for a student, and teaching is never more than the promotion of opportunities, and support for learning.

Constructivism is well established in the literature across a range of educational areas. It is, however, a 'broad church' that contains many sects (Phillips, 1995). These sectarian differences derive in part from the histories and traditions of the different subject areas. In mathematics, for instance, the 'radical constructivism' of Ernst von Glasersfeld (see, for instance, von Glasersfeld, 1993) grew out of philosophical considerations about the nature of knowledge. Von Glasersfeld argues not only that knowledge is actively constructed by the learner, but that the knowledge we build up should be thought of as having an adaptive purpose, to help us operate in the world, rather than being viewed as the discovery of an underlying reality. Radical constructivism denies the possibility of the world being directly 'known', or of knowledge being directly transferred between teacher and learner. While this version of constructivism is not necessarily contradictory to the science education view of constructivism, it is more aggressive in the way it casts the real nature of learning and knowledge. In science education, constructivism grew out of the need to interpret the findings of research on students' conceptions, and from the beginning has had a more pragmatic feel.

Constructivism has, over the last decade, attracted some vociferous critics. For instance, sections of the science and the education communities have argued that the view that students construct coherent 'alternative frameworks' gives too much credence to students' ideas,

and leads to a downgrading of science understandings as 'just another viewpoint' alongside the many that students may come up with. Other critics question the effectiveness of constructivist teaching strategies, given their time-consuming nature. Indeed, constructivist writers vary considerably on the time they recommend that teachers spend exploring and negotiating understandings with students, as against representing the science view directly. Some of this debate is complicated by a blending of constructivist views with earlier 'progressive' traditions (which are related to the work of John Dewey, dating from the 1930s), or with notions of 'discovery' or 'hands-on learning'. In science, the uptake of constructivist ideas is strongly linked to the need to make sense of the findings of the student conceptions research, in contrast to the more theoretical/philosophical emphasis in mathematics education. Nevertheless, within both traditions, constructivist views of learning have been influential in shaping approaches to teaching and learning.

SHIFTS TOWARDS A MORE SOCIAL CONSTRUCTIVIST PERSPECTIVE

Within the constructivist perspective itself, the ground has been shifting. There is a substantial body of critique of both the earlier constructivist literature and the conceptual change literature, pointing out the narrowness of this purely conceptual view of learning and its excessive focus on the learner at the expense of the teacher and the classroom. Within the broad constructivist position, there have been a number of writers calling for the inclusion of broader perspectives than the purely conceptual—for instance, student views of the nature of knowledge (see Chapter 1) and learning. Driver et al. (1996) argue for the importance for learning of students' reasoning strategies, and their views on knowledge production and the nature of science. Other writers have also emphasised the importance of affective factors—interest and motivation, for instance—arguing against 'cold conceptual change' views that students can be convinced to adopt new perspectives through primarily rational means (Sinatra, 2005). Treagust and Duit (2008) review the many changes that are now accommodated within conceptual change perspectives as a result of new research findings on learning. These include the realisation that conceptual change can involve changes in understanding of science knowledge-building processes such as the role of models; that changes in perspective do not only involve rational thinking but also involve affective factors and classroom settings; and that change may take place over quite long periods. They propose a multi-perspective view of conceptual change, including the need to draw on a number of dimensions beyond the strictly conceptual, and link this with recent interest in scientific literacy. This more contemporary focus on student attitudes, and on the role of modelling and analogy in the learning process, is linked with increasing interest in the role of language and literacy in learning science, and on forms of reasoning other than the strictly formal.

Recently there has been much greater interest in exploring learning as a social or cultural phenomenon, with a shift in focus from individual students' understandings to the ways in which classroom environments support effective learning. A social constructivist position focuses our attention on the social processes operating in the classroom by which a teacher promotes a community in which students and the teacher 'co-construct' knowledge. The aim of science or mathematics education then becomes the establishment within the class of shared meanings (Driver et al., 1994). In this process, the teacher represents the very powerful discourses (discussions about thoughts and ideas) of the scientific culture, and scientific ways of viewing and dealing with the world.

In a sense, social constructivist perspectives put the teacher back in the picture, compared with what many felt was a tendency within radical and personal constructivist positions to write the teacher out of the learning process. There have, in fact, been interpretations of personal constructivism that promote a pure form of 'discovery learning' in which the teacher never tells a student anything, but simply organises enabling activities and throws questions back as the responsibility of the learner. This has never been a mainstream position. By making the classroom our focus of attention, we can talk about the way a teacher might frame a learning environment, whereas a purely personal constructivist position can only really make sense of what a teacher does in relation to each individual student.

There has been a strand of thinking in Britain that has encouraged teachers to plan learning programs for each student individually, depending on their needs. This idea grew originally out of Piagetian theory in the 1970s, but was taken up with personal constructivist justifications in the late 1980s. Probing of individual conceptions becomes a central activity in each teaching and learning sequence. The

problem with this approach is twofold. First, any really effective probe of student ideas will throw up so many that it is difficult for teachers to deal with them individually. Second, it is extremely difficult to deal with an alternative perspective if we have in mind the idea of a 'gap' across which we must bring students to the scientists' perspective. Learning is more complex than that. Teachers would often simply ignore the preconceived views and fall back on transmissive approaches (traditional 'chalk and talk', for example).

Social constructivist views emphasise that teachers need to operate with classrooms as much as with individual students. The task for teachers, from this perspective, is to set up the conditions for high-level discussion within the class, through challenging activities, through scaffolding the language and the ideas students have access to, and through promoting conditions for students to feel comfortable about actively sharing and critiquing ideas to arrive at agreed, 'co-constructed' explanations. In such a 'community of inquiry', individual conceptual positions tend to surface and are negotiated as part of the discussion.

Consistent with this perspective, researchers such as Mortimer and Scott (2003) argue that the key to understanding effective science teaching and learning is classroom discourse: the pattern of teacher and student talk during science lessons. One instance is a lesson in which Year 9 students were each given a nail and challenged to put it somewhere to rust (Scott, 1998). When students brought the nails back for display, the classroom discussion switched between sequences that were open and exploratory, and in which students threw in lots of ideas, and sequences where the teacher controlled the conversation more strongly to bring these ideas together. The ability to shift between these different discourse modes is an important aspect of effective teaching. Hackling, Smith and Murcia (2010) link these different types of talk to phases of inquiry within a conceptual change approach. They argue that open, exploratory talk should be the basis of the 'engage' and 'explore' phases of an inquiry approach, whereas the 'explain' phase, in which the teacher brings these ideas together to establish the scientific view, will involve more controlled, 'authoritative' discourse patterns.

SOCIO-CULTURAL PERSPECTIVES

Corresponding to social constructivist perspectives, there has been growing interest in theories of learning that give a more fundamental role to language and culture in the construction of knowledge and even the way we think. Lev Vygotsky's (a Russian psychologist, 1896–1934) ideas have provided a framework to argue for the central role of discourses and communities in knowledge production. From a Vygotskian perspective, thinking and learning are 'mediated' by language and other resources and practices within the classroom. The teacher inducts students into the use of these resources and supports them to become increasingly competent in their use. Learning about chemical reactions, for example, involves learning the language of bonding, equations and electron transfer, as well as the experimental practices, and stories of the history of the development of these ideas and the ways in which they are applied. The specialised language of science, such as chemical equations, acts as a 'mediator' in conceptual learning—the terms are both the pathway to conceptual understanding and the way we express the understanding.

The theoretical perspectives built around this idea of mediation are more broadly known as 'socio-cultural'. This term can be understood roughly to correspond to 'social constructivism', but does not limit its focus to classroom interactions. A socio-cultural perspective takes the more fundamental position that knowledge and learning should be seen in terms of increasing access to and competence with ways of talking and acting within the wider discourse community of science. From this perspective, quality learning involves students in increasingly mastering and coordinating these 'discursive' resources to develop explanations, interpret evidence and solve problems. Learning is seen as a process of *enculturation*, involving increasing capacity to *participate* in scientific ways of talking and acting rather than as the *acquisition* of mental structures that reside in our heads.

In the classroom environment implied by a socio-cultural perspective, language is central, involving negotiation between the teacher's and the students' language resources to achieve shared meaning. The teacher scaffolds students to become increasingly independent members of the discourse community. In fact, many of the conceptual change teaching schemes, dating from the 1980s, incorporate very similar principles.

Scientific literacy and representations perspectives

There is growing acceptance of scientific literacy as a fundamental aim of school science, to prepare students for an adulthood in which they can interpret and reason with the ideas of science. Norris and Phillips (2003) argue that this involves students acquiring literacy in the sense of being able to use the specific languages of science, which are fundamental to acquiring scientific understandings and skills. There is a growing consensus that learning science involves students gaining access to a range of subject-specific and general representational tools used by the scientific community to construct knowledge about the natural world (Moje, 2008). Doing science involves working with rich and multi-modal representations such as diagrams, models, graphs and tables, or animations. These are powerful resources for speculating, reasoning, developing explanations, theory-building and communicating within the science community and more broadly. Becoming 'literate' in science therefore involves being able to generate and coordinate a range of representational resources to work and think scientifically: to learn the multiple ways of 'knowing, doing, believing and communicating' in the subject (Moje, 2008, p. 4). Tytler and Prain (2010) have argued that the learning difficulties identified so comprehensively in the conceptual change literature are in fact representational challenges, and that a scientific literacy perspective can provide ways forward for supporting quality learning in science.

For teachers, a scientific literacy perspective implies that we should focus primarily on supporting students to learn the conventions associated with different types of representations, and to coordinate and problem-solve effectively with them. There are two approaches to this. One is to support students being able to interpret standard science representations and their conventions, such as chemical models or the ways graphs are presented and used. The other is to build teaching sequences in which students are guided to construct their own scientific representations based on the argument that it is only by being immersed in the discursive practices of science that they can really learn how they work. Researchers have identified key principles for student learning through such a representation-construction approach: (1) identification of the representations needed to work with key science ideas; (2) a focus on the way representations work—the conventions, their function and their purpose—through explicit classroom discussion; (3) sequencing of challenges where students generate representations, critique, negotiate and refine these, and coordinate them where appropriate with strong perceptual contexts (hands-on, activity based); and (4) ongoing assessment as teachers and students make judgements about the adequacy of the generated representations and their relation to the 'authorised' representational conventions.

As an example of a scientific literacy and representation approach, Figure 2.1 shows two lower secondary school students' work when (a) they were challenged to represent what they imagine happens at the particle level to explain the stretch of a rubber band, and (b) how they might represent the difference between 'revolve' and 'rotate' in planetary motion. What factors in these representations help you to understand what the students are thinking? How would you approach teaching these students about these science ideas?

FIGURE 2.1: Student-generated representations in response to a challenge

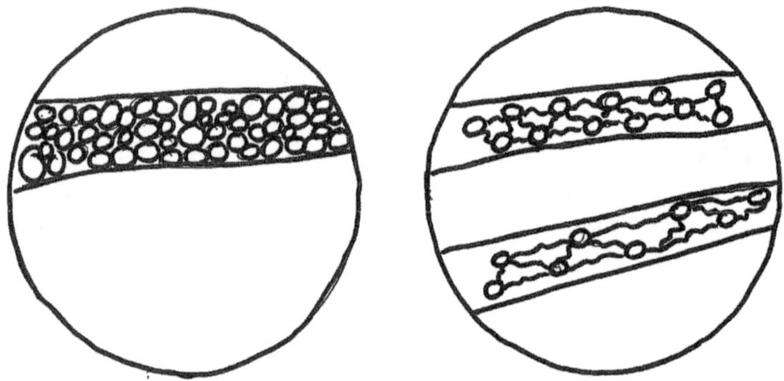

(a) Particles in a rubber band before stretching (on the left) and during stretching (on the right)

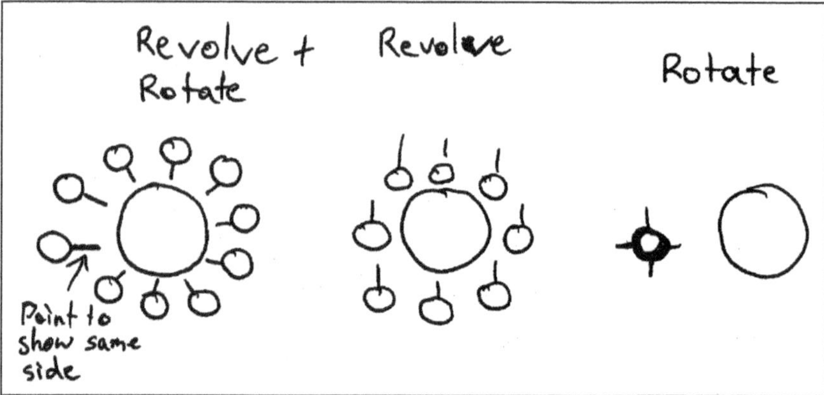

(b) The difference between 'revolve' and 'rotate' in planetary motion

Situated cognition perspective

A socio-cultural perspective that emphasises the contexts of learning is the *situated cognition* perspective. Rogoff and Lave (1984) argue that context is an integral aspect of what we learn; the situations in which an understanding is generated are an integral part of that understanding. Illustrative of this view are studies on young children in South America which highlighted the fact that children who are incompetent at mathematics in school can operate with extraordinarily sophisticated numerical procedures while operating as street vendors. In fact, more or less from the beginning of science education research into student conceptions, it was realised that the context in which explanations were generated would affect the ideas that were used. Joan Solomon (1983) described the way that real-world contexts triggered different views and explanations of energy, compared with when the question was asked in a classroom context. She was able to show that, over time, the scientists' view of energy that was learned in school was abandoned and that everyday forms of knowledge reasserted themselves outside the influence of the science classroom.

Children often compartmentalise what they learn in our classrooms as 'school knowledge', and treat it as irrelevant to more general situations. Knowledge generated in a classroom is fundamentally a response to, and a product of, that situation. To put the case more broadly, there is no such thing as a universal understanding, separate from the social/cultural framework within which it was generated. The implication that must be drawn from this insight is that, if school knowledge is to be useful to learners out there in the world, continual links must be made between school experience and social uses of the science knowledge. We must break down the boundaries between the classroom and the real world.

SUMMARY OF KEY POINTS

So where have we got with our quest to clarify what the pathway to a meaningful understanding of science might be? It seems clear that it involves students in some sort of shift in perspective from their existing understanding to a scientific understanding, and that this involves challenging their existing ideas. It seems clear that this process is gradual, and involves students learning to use both scientific and everyday ideas in a range of situations and to recognise how they interrelate. It involves the engagement of students in a process of shared meaning-making, guided by the teacher. It involves mastery of the discourses of science—including natural language—of ways of questioning and arguing and linking ideas with evidence, and of co-ordinating representations and artefacts in a shared enterprise. It involves linking classroom science with students' lives outside the classroom. Chapters 3 and 4 will examine different science teaching and learning schemes based on these ideas.

DISCUSSION QUESTIONS

2.1 'They must have learned this! I distinctly remember teaching it to them!' How would you respond to such an assertion?

2.2 Constructivist perspectives emphasise that responsibility for learning resides with the learner. What, therefore, is the role of the teacher? To what extent might it be appropriate or effective to 'tell' students about science concepts?

2.3 There have been much-quoted debates in the research community about whether learning is better viewed as 'acquisition' or 'participation'. Are these metaphors for learning necessarily opposed? In what senses might both have something to offer?

2.4 Socio-cultural theories view knowledge as situated, in an important sense, in the conversations and shared meanings developed in classrooms or groups, supported by the materials and representational artefacts used by students and teachers. How do you think understandings of a student in a classroom would relate to the understandings he or she might demonstrate a few days later, on their own? In what sense might they be or not be the same?

2.5 The literacy perspectives described in this chapter are part of a general perspective on knowledge as 'text based'. Do you think there are understandings we might have that are separate from the representational means by which we might communicate them—for example, in what sense can we understand 'animal diversity' without drawing on classification schemes?

REFERENCES

Bell, B. (1993). *Children's science, constructivism and learning in science.* Geelong: Deakin University Press.

Carey, S. (1985). *Conceptual change in childhood.* Cambridge, MA: MIT Press.

Cosgrove, M., & Osborne, R. (1985). Lesson frameworks for changing children's ideas. In R. Osborne & P. Freyberg (Eds.), *Learning in science: The implications of children's science* (pp. 101–111). Auckland: Heinemann.

Driver, R., Asoko, H., Leach, J., Mortimer, E., & Scott, P. (1994). Constructing scientific knowledge in the classroom. *Educational Researcher, 23*(7), 5–12.

Driver, R., Leach, J., Millar, R., & Scott, P. (1996). *Young people's images of science.* Milton Keynes: Open University Press.

Hackling, M., Smith, P., & Murcia, K. (2010). Talking science: Developing a discourse of inquiry. *Teaching Science, 56*(1), 17–22.

Kuhn, T. S. (1970). *The structure of scientific revolutions* (2nd ed.). Chicago: University of Chicago Press.

Moje, E. (2008). Foregrounding the disciplines in secondary literacy teaching and learning: A call for change. *Journal of Adolescent and Adult Literacy, 52*, 96–107.

Mortimer, E., & Scott, P. (2003). *Making meaning in secondary science classrooms.* Maidenhead: Open University Press.

Norris, S., & Phillips, L. (2003). How literacy in its fundamental sense is central to scientific literacy. *Science Education, 87*, 224–240.

Phillips, D. (1995). The good, the bad and the ugly: The many faces of constructivism. *Educational Researcher, 24*(7), 5–12.

Rogoff, B., & Lave, J. (Eds.). (1984). *Everyday cognition: Its development in social context.* Cambridge, MA: Harvard University Press.

Scott, P. (1998). Teacher talk and meaning making in science classrooms: A Vygotskian analysis and review. *Studies in Science Education, 32*, 45–80.

Sinatra, G. (2005). The 'warming trend' in conceptual change research: The legacy of Paul R. Pintrich. *Educational Psychologist, 40*(2), 107–115.

Solomon, J. (1983). Learning about energy: How pupils think in two domains. *European Journal of Science Education, 5*(1), 49–59.

Treagust, D., & Duit, R. (2008). Conceptual change: A discussion of theoretical, methodological and practical challenges for science education. *Cultural Studies of Science Education, 3*, 297–328.

Tytler, R. (1998). The nature of students' informal science conceptions. *International Journal of Science Education, 20*(8), 901–927.

Tytler, R., & Prain, V. (2010). A framework for re-thinking learning in science from recent cognitive science perspectives. *International Journal of Science Education, 32*(15), 2055–2078.

von Glasersfeld, E. (1993). Questions and answers about radical constructivism. In K. Tobin (Ed.), *The practice of constructivism in science education* (pp. 23–38). Hillsdale, NJ: Lawrence Erlbaum.

CHAPTER THREE

CONCEPTUAL CHANGE LEARNING AND TEACHING

David Treagust and Reinders Duit

OUTCOMES

By the end of this chapter you will be able to:

- Distinguish between different types of conceptual change
- Describe and illustrate different approaches for teaching for conceptual change
- Describe and illustrate how you can know that student learning undergoes conceptual change

INTRODUCTION

Research on students' and teachers' conceptions of, and their roles in teaching and learning, science has become one of the most important research domains in science education and has a rich history in Australia and New Zealand. From a teaching perspective, the findings from conceptual change research provide a large number of avenues for instruction.

This chapter is divided into four parts: the first describes the main issues behind the notion of conceptual change; the second describes three different theoretical perspectives of conceptual change with examples drawn from science classroom research; the third provides a discussion of how teachers can engage students in science so that they may experience conceptual change; and the fourth and final part provides a summary of the key points.

THE MAIN ISSUES BEHIND CONCEPTUAL CHANGE

There are eight main issues behind the notion of conceptual change:

1. Students are not simply passive learners but make sense of new information in terms of their previous ideas and experiences, which may lead to scientific knowledge or intuitive knowledge that has been called *children's science*. This is the essential feature of the theory of constructivism.
2. Consequently, students attend science classes with pre-instructional knowledge or beliefs about the phenomena and concepts to be taught that are frequently not in harmony with science views and the teacher's intended instruction.
3. Students' knowledge is often fragmented, and if this knowledge is to be built coherently then students need to be intellectually engaged.
4. Students build their own knowledge. Recent studies on conceptual change emphasise the importance of the role of the learner, suggesting that the learner can play an active, intentional role in the process of knowledge restructuring.
5. In a general sense, conceptual change denotes learning pathways from students' pre-instructional conceptions to the science concepts to be learned.
6. Changes that lead to learning can be minor or major. There are two types of conceptual change, variously called weak knowledge restructuring–assimilation or conceptual capture–and strong/radical knowledge restructuring–accommodation or conceptual exchange.
7. The term 'conceptual change' is used for learning when the pre-instructional conceptual structures of the learners are fundamentally restructured in order to allow a deeper understanding of the intended science concepts under consideration.

8. The term 'conceptual change' has been given various meanings; change often has been misunderstood as being a simple exchange of pre-instructional conceptions for the science concepts.

DIFFERENT THEORETICAL PERSPECTIVES OF CONCEPTUAL CHANGE

For more than three decades, researchers have investigated students' pre-instructional conceptions and conceptual change in various science content areas such as the electric circuit, force, refraction, energy, combustion, photosynthesis and respiration, chemical equilibrium and evolution (Duit, 2009). Through this research, it has become evident that to better understand learning we need to think about conceptual change from various theoretical perspectives. This chapter considers three of these theoretical perspectives. The first is an *epistemological* perspective—that is, we will consider how students think about the status of their knowledge. The second perspective is an *ontological* perspective, through which we will consider how students think about the nature of things in the world around them. The third perspective is an *affective* perspective, enabling us to consider how the students feel about the knowledge and the learning process. While the jargon can be challenging, these theoretical perspectives help us understand conceptual change learning. In the following sections, we elaborate on and provide classroom snapshots to illustrate these perspectives.

An epistemological perspective of conceptual change: How students view the status of their conceptual knowledge

The best-known conceptual change model in science education is based on examining how students consider the status of their conceptual knowledge—that is, an epistemological perspective (Posner et al., 1982). In this conceptual change model, student dissatisfaction with a pre-instructional conception indicates it has low status. Such dissatisfaction is believed to initiate an awareness by the student that a change in conceptualisation is needed. If the learner is dissatisfied with their pre-instructional conception and it has low status, it then becomes possible for the teacher to introduce and increase the status of the scientific concept in the student's mind. We use the words *intelligible*, *plausible* and *fruitful* to describe increasing levels of status of a conception. An intelligible conception is sensible if it is non-contradictory and its meaning is understood by the student; plausible means that in addition to the student knowing what the conception means, the student finds the conception believable; and the conception is fruitful if it helps the learner solve other problems or suggests new research directions. The extent to which the conception meets these conditions is termed the status of a learner's conception. Ideally, teachers should aim to have scientific conceptions become intelligible, plausible and fruitful for their students. Conceptual changes may be permanent or temporary, and the higher the status of the conception, the more likely it is that conceptual change has taken place.

Sometimes students can hold two or more conceptions at the same time. When competing conceptions are incompatible, two things may happen. If the new conception achieves higher status than the pre-instructional conception, conceptual change may occur. If the pre-instructional conception retains higher status, conceptual change will not proceed for the time being. It should be remembered that a replaced conception is not forgotten, and the learner may wholly or partly reinstate it at a later date because the learner, not the teacher, makes the decisions about the status of the new concept and any conceptual changes. In this manner, the learner can play an active, intentional role in the process of conceptual change. Snapshot 3.1 provides an example of where an analogy used by the teacher in an optics class helped to improve the conceptual status of a scientific explanation of refraction.

SNAPSHOT 3.1: Understanding an optics lesson by using an epistemological perspective of conceptual change

In this optics class, the teacher demonstrated the path taken by a beam of light as it passed obliquely from air into a rectangular glass block and then emerged from the glass block parallel to the original beam but displaced sideways. The teacher explained that the bending occurred because the light slowed down when it entered the glass and sped up when it emerged. Many of the students found it difficult to understand why the ray of light bent when it entered and exited the glass block. To show why the change in speed produced a change in direction, the teacher compared the beam of light to the wheels of a small, two-wheeled cart as it rolled obliquely from a hard to a softer surface. This type of comparison is called an analogy (for full details, see Harrison and Treagust, 1993). The teacher explained that the axle of the wheel is like the wave front of the beam of light. She said that when one wheel entered the soft surface it slowed down, causing the cart to skew slightly, changing its direction. The teacher demonstrated this effect using a set of wheels moving at an angle from a hard surface on to carpet.

To help us understand what the students were thinking during this teaching sequence, we gave them a worksheet and interviewed some students in an in-depth way. The worksheet and interview included questions based on activities that had been completed in the classroom. Students were asked to draw and verbalise their predictions—for example, when light shines through a glass block—and were encouraged to give their reasons. Extension questions such as, 'How would you explain that to a friend?' were included to encourage the students to reflect upon their own conceptions and to help us work out the status of the students' conceptions—that is, we worked out whether the students' understanding of refraction was intelligible, plausible and/or fruitful for them. We discovered that the students who were taught using the analogy with the wheels had higher status conceptions than a comparable group of students who were taught by the same teacher without the analogy. The findings indicated that the wheels analogy was a useful teaching tool to support conceptual change, and increased the status of the students' conceptions of refraction.

An ontological perspective of conceptual change: How students view the nature of the world

How a learner views the material world can have an impact on learning; such views of the material world are referred to as ontology—the ways in which different entities exist and how they are grouped depending on their behaviour (Chi, 2008). We can think about and ask ontological questions about scientific entities such as: Is it matter or is it a process? Is it concrete or abstract? Is it local or global? Scientists often understand scientific phenomena to be in different ontological categories when compared with many students' pre-instructional conceptions. Heat, for example, has various meanings in colloquial language. It may denote comparably high temperatures (e.g. when it is claimed that the heat today is hard to bear) or something material stored in hot objects. In physics, heat is conceptualised as a flow of energy in transit from a hot object to a colder one due to the temperature differences—a process, not a material. Likewise, discussion of a gene in daily life often invokes the meaning of an inherited trait such as the shape of a nose or the colour of a flower—a physical entity—whereas in genetics, a gene is conceptualised as a biochemical process. Research has shown that conceptual change often involves a student rethinking the ontology of a scientific idea. For example, they might have to stop thinking of heat as a substance and think of it as a process. Snapshot 3.2 provides an example of how an ontological perspective can help us understand conceptual change when secondary students learn chemical equilibrium.

SNAPSHOT 3.2: An example that illustrates how an ontological perspective helps us to understand conceptual change when students learn chemical equilibrium

An investigation by Chiu, Chou and Liu (2002), designed to examine how students learned and constructed understanding of chemical equilibrium, compared students in a classroom that included conceptual change teaching strategies such as coaching, modelling, scaffolding, articulation, reflection and exploration with those taught by a teacher who incorporated traditional teaching strategies such as lecturing and demonstrations. Based on an ontological perspective of conceptual change, the researchers hypothesised that the dynamic, process nature of chemical equilibrium, which is impossible for students to observe, prevented them from deeply understanding this concept.

Both groups of students' understanding of chemical equilibrium before instruction were similar—they lacked knowledge of definitions (closed/open systems), of the nature of chemical equilibrium (dynamic movement) and of the constraints of chemical equilibrium. One activity was designed for students to develop an understanding of the dynamic nature of chemical reactions. The initial question stated:

Consider the following reversible reaction. Dilute aqueous potassium thiocyanate (KSCN) is sometimes used for blood effects in television, film and theatre. It can be kept as a colourless solution. When it comes in contact with ferric ions (e.g. when mixed with ferric chloride or ferric nitrate), the product of the reaction is a blood red colour, due to the formation of the thiocyantoiron complex ion:

$$Fe^{3+}(aq) + SCN^{-}(aq) \rightleftharpoons FeSCN^{2+}(aq)$$

Yellow Colourless Red

When Fe^{3+} and SCN^{-} are combined, equilibrium is established between these two ions and the $FeSCN^{2+}$ ion.

What would be observed if two drops of potassium thiocyanate (KSCN) and two drops of ferric (iron) nitrate ($Fe(NO_3)_3$) were added to an aqueous solution?

Changing the concentrations of the ions will change the equilibrium, the concentration of all substances will redistribute and a new equilibrium will be achieved with different concentrations of reactants and products. The addition of more Fe^{3+} and SCN^{-} causes the equilibrium to shift in favour of the products and more of the complex is formed, turning the solution to a deeper red. This means the solution can change from colourless to red and vice versa.

Students find it difficult to understand a solution in equilibrium as a dynamic process. An ontological perspective of conceptual change can be used to explain students' difficulty. In order to understand the equation and problems above, the students had to stop thinking about the solution as a static substance and think about it as a dynamic process. Students in the conceptual change group were more able to develop their ideas about the sub-microscopic concepts that explain the dynamic equilibrium compared with the lecturing-demonstration group, and were able to comprehend that the added compounds were eliminated by the reaction that they themselves had caused as well as the macroscopic phenomenon of equilibrium evidenced in the reaction.

An affective perspective of conceptual change: How students feel about science and learning science

Learning is never solely a mere cognitive concern; affective issues always play a significant role. Science teachers know very well that students' interests, enjoyment, willingness, intentions, needs and motivation for learning science are important issues to consider in the classroom because they are indications of how students perceive the lesson being taught. These affective aspects of learning are the third perspective of conceptual change considered in this chapter. In a review of linking the cognitive and the emotional in teaching and learning science, some researchers argue that it is necessary to develop a unity between the cognitive and emotional dimensions such that emotions and cognitive outcomes have equal status in the lessons. This means that instruction should not only focus on developing cognitive issues (like understanding concepts, principles and views of the nature of science) but also include affective variables like enhancing students' interests and motivation. Chapter 9 provides considerable information about student engagement and motivation in science.

Multi-dimensional perspectives of conceptual change

It seems obvious that taking into account only one of the three approaches to conceptual change may provide a limited understanding of student learning. Consequently, there are a growing number of multi-dimensional approaches to conceptual change that have promise for improving science teaching and learning. In brief, multi-dimensional perspectives of conceptual change that consider epistemological, ontological and affective domains need to be employed in order to adequately address the complexity of the teaching and learning processes. Only such frameworks can sufficiently model the teaching and learning processes that exist in the classroom. As stated above, much of the research on conceptual change has taken a particular perspective, namely an epistemological perspective, an ontological perspective or an affective perspective, but there is ample evidence in research on learning and instruction that the cognitive and affective issues are closely linked. Snapshot 3.3 provides an example of where a multi-dimensional perspective helped us to understand conceptual change learning in genetics.

SNAPSHOT 3.3: An example in genetics that illustrates how a multi-dimensional perspective helps us to understand conceptual change

Venville and Treagust (1998) examined changes in Year 10 students' conceptions of genes during a ten-week genetics course. Data collected from student worksheets given before and after the course, lesson observations, recordings of classroom discourse and student interviews at the end of the course were interpreted using a multi-dimensional framework of conceptual change from epistemological, ontological and affective perspectives. From an epistemological perspective, students' conceptions were classified as being intelligible, plausible and/or fruitful. Students' ontological conceptions of genes developed from the idea that a gene is a passive particle passed from parents to offspring (a material) to being a more active particle that controls characteristics. However, the desired idea that a gene is a section of DNA that is a code for the transcription and translation of an amino acid (a process) did not become plausible for the majority of students. From an affective perspective, it was evident that even though the students stated that they enjoyed the genetics course and were observed to participate in classroom activities, they had less interest in the sub-microscopic explanatory mechanisms of genetics. They were not very interested in topics such as DNA structure, replication, transcription and translation, preferring to use simple Mendelian genetics to try to answer questions about their own physical characteristics. Overall, despite the intent of the teacher, the teaching approaches did not encourage a sophisticated conception of a gene in the minds of the majority of students.

TEACHING FOR CONCEPTUAL CHANGE

In this section, we describe four ways in which teachers can enhance the opportunities for students to experience conceptual change: (1) being aware of students' conceptual frameworks; (2) using cognitive conflict such as the Predict-Observe-Explain sequence; (3) using analogies; and (4) focusing on modelling and linking explanations at different levels.

Being aware of students' pre-instructional understandings

Many teachers are intuitively constructivist in their approach to teaching—for example, they want to be able to assist students in their learning, and they are aware of the importance of students' cognitive activity and observations. However, some teachers identify themselves as mediators of facts and information, and are not aware of students' ways of interpreting the world and the role of students' pre-instructional conceptions. These teachers often think that good instruction is only indicated by students performing well on school tests or external examinations. Being aware of students' pre-instructional understandings and how they impact on learning is an important first step to becoming an excellent 'constructivist' science teacher. This awareness opens teachers' minds; it helps them listen to their students and it helps them to start thinking about ways that they can take their students' pre-instructional conceptions into consideration when planning and teaching.

Using cognitive conflict such as the Predict–Observe–Explain sequence

One way in which teachers can teach for conceptual change is to incorporate strategies into their teaching repertoires that overtly provide insights into students' pre-instructional understanding of the scientific phenomenon being examined. One such strategy is the Predict–Observe–Explain sequence, which is both a probe to expose students' pre-instructional knowledge and a teaching strategy. In this teaching strategy, students are presented with an event that may be an experiment or a demonstration, and are asked to predict the outcome. They then conduct the experiment or observe the demonstration and make observations. Finally, students explain their observations in relation to their predictions. Sometimes the prediction and observation will be consistent and other times they will not. When they are not consistent, we can say cognitive conflict has occurred because the students' predictions, based on their pre-instructional understanding, conflict with their observations. This is a very powerful strategy because it can make students dissatisfied with their pre-instructional conceptions and lower their status, making the students more receptive to scientific explanations.

The Predict-Observe-Explain sequence reflects how a constructivist view of learning can be used in a classroom situation for teaching heat and expansion of liquids. Heat is experienced by students at a very early age, and it is likely that experience with situations involving heat and expansion form the basis of pre-instructional knowledge or beliefs. As noted above, the ontological aspect of the concept of heat can create learning difficulties. The topic of heat and expansion of liquids taught in a high school physics class lends itself well to the POE sequence, and this approach is elaborated further in Snapshot 3.4.

SNAPSHOT 3.4: Using the POE teaching strategy for conceptual change about heat

A Predict-Observe-Explain strategy can be used by teachers to help students understand the concept of heat. This involves an experiment on the expansion of coloured water in glass tubing fitted to a flask, to be conducted by groups of two students (see the equipment illustrated below). When the flask is plunged into hot water, the level of the coloured water in the glass tubing first falls slightly and then starts to rise steadily. The initial fall in level of the water is not expected by the students, and is caused by the expansion of the glass of the flask, which becomes heated and expands before the heat has time to be conducted through the glass into the coloured water. The water level later rises as the liquid becomes heated and expands. The unexpected initial observation causes cognitive conflict for many students.

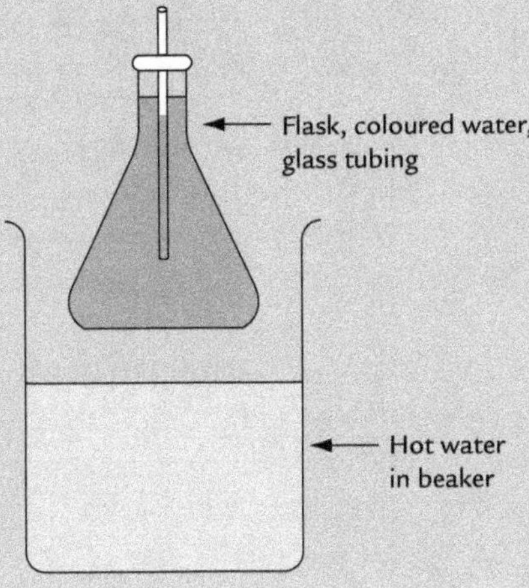

The three phases of the POE activity are explained below.

Predict

The lesson begins with the teacher showing the class some glass tubing fitted to a flask filled with coloured water. Students are independently asked to write down their answers to the following question:

1. Predict what will happen to the water level in the glass tubing if the flask is plunged into the hot water from the initial moment and onwards? State and explain the reason(s) for your prediction.

Observe and explain

The next stage of the teaching sequence involves the students performing the experiment in groups of two. The flask is then plunged into the beaker of hot water. The students are requested to independently write down their observations by answering the following question:

2. What happened to the water level in the glass tubing when the flask was immersed into the hot water from the initial moment and onwards? State and explain the reason(s) for your observations.

In the course of the experiment, students make independent observations while sharing the apparatus in groups of two with no discussions allowed. In the next stage, students are asked to make comparisons between their own predictions and their observations by answering the following question:

3. Compare your observation with your prediction. Are they in agreement or disagreement? Explain with your reason(s).

Finally, students are asked to discuss their answers to the three questions in groups, after which they each write down their final reasons and explanations.

The Predict–Observe–Explain teaching sequence illustrates how students' pre-instructional knowledge and beliefs can affect their observations and interpretations of new learning. In the Predict-Observe-Explain presented in Snapshot 3.4, the majority of students typically predict and 'observe' an initial rise of the water level in the glass tubing. Reasons and explanations are personal constructions generated from previous experiences and learning. Personally constructed alternative conceptions to explain observations, such as 'water only expands when it freezes', 'water expands when water pressure increases', 'molecules are more energetic and collide more frequently' and 'the squashy molecule model' demonstrate students' lack of understanding about macroscopic concepts of liquid expansion and the sub-microscopic concept of the kinetic theory of matter. The Predict-Observe-Explain teaching sequence does create the opportunity for some students to reconstruct and change their pre-instructional conceptions as a result of inconsistencies and/or contradictions between observations and predictions, and hence undergo conceptual change.

Using analogies

Analogies are used in everyday life to help explain various phenomena—for example, we might say 'the shirt fits like a glove'. Science teachers also use analogies to explain things to students; an example is when we say that a *lock and key* is an analogy for enzyme action. The target is the science concept—enzyme action; the analogy is the everyday event of a lock and a key. There are different types of analogy, including verbal, pictorial, personal, bridging and multiple analogies (see Aubusson, Treagust & Harrison, 2009). When the teacher provides verbal analogies in class, the students are left to work out the comparisons and conclusions about the target (i.e. the science concept) from the description of the analogy. Pictorial analogies presented by the teacher or in a texbook better highlight the desired features of an analogy. This visualisation reduces the likelihood that the student is not sufficiently familiar with the analogy.

Personal analogies assist students by relating abstract scientific concepts to concepts familiar to students, such as people, money, food and relationships. Students can be physically involved in a personal analogy by, for example, being in a role-play where they walk around the classroom in such a manner that their direction of travel is analogous to the motion of electrons through a wire or ionic migration through a solution during electrolysis. Alternatively, the students may only be involved at a mental level—in other words, they have to use their imagination to work out the events.

From a teaching perspective, the use of analogies can enhance conceptual change learning since they open new perspectives and can be motivational in that, as the teacher uses ideas from the students' real-world experience, a sense of intrinsic interest is generated. The presentation of a concrete analogy facilitates understanding of abstract concepts by pointing to the similarities between objects or events in the students' world and the phenomenon under discussion. In addition, when teachers use analogies, this creates an increased awareness on the part of the teacher that they need to take students' pre-instructional conceptions into consideration when teaching.

Despite the advantages and usefulness of analogies, using this teaching tool can cause incorrect or impaired learning. For example, the analogy may be unfamiliar to the learner. Moreover, if the students lack visual imagery, analogical reasoning or correlational reasoning, then the value of analogies may be limited. For students who are capable of understanding a direct explanation of an abstract scientific idea, the inclusion of an analogy might add unnecessary information. For these reasons, some teachers choose not to use analogies at all and thereby avoid these problems, while at the same time forsaking the advantages of analogy use.

No analogy shares all its attributes with the target, or by definition it would become an example. Attributes that are not similar between analogy and the target often cause misunderstanding for learners. Another related constraint occurs when the students attempt to transfer ideas from the analogy to the target in an inappropriate manner. If analogies are to be used more effectively by science teachers, a carefully planned strategy is required that makes the analogies relevant to as many students as possible. One approach for using analogies involves the three phases of Focus, Action, and Reflection (FAR); it has come to be known as the FAR Guide (see Figure 3.1). Typical lessons using the FAR Guide in biology, chemistry and physics can be found in Coll and Harrison (2008). An example of the use of the FAR Guide for teaching about chemical bonding is provided in Snapshot 3.5.

Using models appropriately and linking between levels of representation

While the macroscopic, observable chemical phenomena are the basis of chemistry, explanations usually rely on models of the sub-microscopic behaviour of particles. Indeed, the use of computer modelling programs or ball-and-stick models that students can handle and visualise has been shown to develop students' understanding of chemical compounds at the sub-microscopic level, and hence result in conceptual change.

FIGURE 3.1: The FAR Guide for teaching and learning science with analogies

Focus	
Concept	Is the science concept difficult, unfamiliar or abstract?
Students	What ideas do the students already have about the concept?
Analogy	Is the analogy something with which students are familiar?
Action	
Likes	Discuss the features of the analogy and the science concept. Draw similarities between them.
Unlikes	Discuss where the analogy is unlike the science concept.
Reflection	
Conclusions	Was the analogy clear and useful, or confusing?
Improvements	Refocus as above in light of the teaching and learning outcomes.

SNAPSHOT 3.5: Using the FAR Guide for a balloon analogy to represent chemical bonds and molecular shapes

The use of the FAR Guide is illustrated in this classroom snapshot, where balloons are used as an analogy for chemical bonds and molecular shapes. The forces between nuclei and electrons resulting in covalent bond formation are purely electrostatic in nature. The valence shell electron pair repulsion (VSEPR) theory is based on the repulsion between electron pairs around a central nucleus producing linear, trigonal planar and tetrahedral molecules in, for example, ethyne, ethene and methane respectively. Students have difficulty visualising repulsion between electron pairs in adjacent covalent bonds. They are, however, familiar with the elasticity of compressed air and balloons.

A simple way to demonstrate the repulsion between adjacent electron pairs is to take four elliptical balloons inflated to their maximum with their stems tied tightly together. Tie a piece of thread to the joined stems and hang the unit from the ceiling. The pneumatic pressure of the balloons will force them into a tetrahedral shape. If one balloon is burst, the remaining three take up a trigonal planar shape and when another balloon is burst, the two remaining balloons become roughly linear, as illustrated below. More information on this analogy can be found in Treagust, Venville and Harrison (2001).

Four balloons in a tetrahedral shape

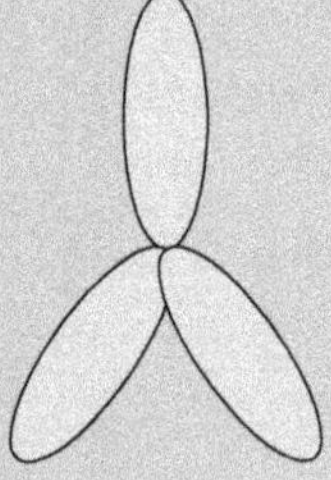

Three balloons in a planar shape

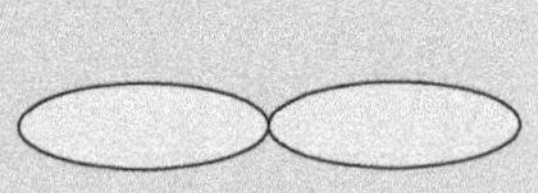

Two balloons in a linear shape

It is important that students are made aware of the limitations of models and the differences between the representations and reality. The extensive and accepted process of using models for explanations has made the models appear as fact to many teachers and students. However, research has shown that students often are unable to differentiate models from the scientific phenomenon that the model is being used to explain (Harrison & Treagust, 1996). Indeed, teachers and textbooks often provide students with representations of atoms and molecules as though they were real and factual. The strengths and limitations of each model need to be discussed.

Research has shown that it is essential for teachers to ensure that their explanations using models are student-friendly and compatible with students' existing knowledge. It is also important for teachers to clearly link different types of models, including symbolic representations such as chemical formula and equations, with sub-microscopic representations such as ball-and-stick models (Gilbert & Treagust, 2009). For example, when science teachers first introduce ball-and-stick models of chemical molecules–typically in Year 8–they should make explicit connections for their students between the components in the molecular model (hydrogen and oxygen atoms, for example), how we represent that in a chemical formula such as H_2O and real water. This approach has been shown to be valuable in explaining the observed, or macro-level, chemical phenomena (such as water or a crystal of salt) and thereby linking all three levels. Unfortunately, teachers often assume that an understanding about how the three levels of representation link together is obvious to students, and when this assumption is not true misunderstandings can eventuate. Consequently, the position of the symbolic representations in relation to the sub-microscopic and macroscopic levels should be discussed clearly in classes.

We investigated Year 11 students' understanding of teaching models used in representing compounds in introductory organic chemistry. During the lessons, students worked with several teaching models, including structural formula, ball-and-stick models, a computer program and space-filling models. The models were used to help determine nomenclature, and the structure and properties of simple organic molecules. While initially using the ball-and-stick model to represent organic hydrocarbons, students became familiar with the bonding rules and constructed feasible compounds. Students observed that no matter how they manipulated the model of hexane, for example, it would not form a 'straight' chain. This observation, along with rotating all the atoms in a compound, made it possible to view the structure from a different perspective, which helped students to understand the significance of the angles between the atoms in the organic compounds. The student discussions we observed indicated that teaching and learning with ball-and-stick models of simple organic molecules served as valid descriptive tools of scientific models and assisted the students in developing their own mental or conceptual models.

CHALLENGES FOR TEACHERS

The main challenge for teachers is how to determine sufficient evidence to identify conceptual change? Some of the most useful information available to teachers about students' achievement and understanding comes from topic tests and examinations, particularly tests at the beginning and end of a topic. However, identifying changes in concepts on a multiple choice test without any additional information to gauge the decisions does not provide useful information about conceptual change. In addition, as was noted in several of the snapshots, it is often the case that more than one source of evidence—for example, classroom observations of students' discussion with the teacher or interviews or responses to a computer simulation—is needed to judge conceptual change.

Successful teaching that results in outcomes of students' conceptual change is a major challenge. Teachers who are better informed about conceptual change are able to appreciate the importance of the epistemological and ontological aspects of scientific concepts and using appropriate teaching strategies, some of which are described in this chapter, to develop practices that enable students to think more clearly about a concept.

SUMMARY OF KEY POINTS

Teaching for conceptual change can be considered from an epistemological perspective (which indicates the status of students' conceptions), an ontological perspective (how students perceive the nature of scientific entities) and students' affective responses to learning (related to their interests, motivation, and attitudes to school and to science). Each of these vantage points is supported by a particular theoretical position. Teachers intend students to learn the planned curriculum but this does not always occur. With a focus on challenging students as they learn a new topic, conceptual change can take place by teachers (1) being aware of students' conceptual frameworks; (2) using cognitive conflict such as the Predict-Observe-Explain sequence; (3) using analogies; and (4) focusing on modelling and explicitly connecting different levels of representation.

DISCUSSION QUESTIONS

3.1 Describe the three types of conceptual change and the ways you can identify them, based on students' responses to the teacher's questions or answers to questions in the textbook.

3.2 Describe at least three approaches to science lessons where you can teach to bring about conceptual change.

3.3 Why does a focus only on test scores not provide a complete picture of learning?

REFERENCES

Aubusson, P., Treagust, D. F., & Harrison, A. G. (2009). Metaphor and analogy in science. In S. M. Ritchie (Ed.), *Science education research in Australasia* (pp. 199–216). Rotterdam: Sense Publishers.

Chi, M. T. H. (2008). Three types of conceptual change: Belief revision, mental model transformation and categorical shift. In S. Vosniadou (Ed.), *International handbook of research on conceptual change* (pp. 61–82). New York: Routledge.

Chiu, M.-H., Chou, C.-C., & Liu, C.-J. (2002). Dynamic processes of conceptual change: Analysis of constructing mental models of chemical equilibrium. *Journal of Research in Science Teaching, 39*, 713–737.

Coll, R. K., & Harrison, A. (Eds.) (2008). *The FAR Guide—an interesting way to teach analogies*. Thousand Oaks, CA: Corwin Press.

Duit, R. (2009). STCSE—Bibliography: Students' and teachers' conceptions and science education. Kiel, Germany: IPN—Leibniz Institute for Science and Mathematics Education. Retrieved 24 November 2011 from http://www.ipn.uni-kiel.de/aktuell/stcse/stcse.html.

Gilbert, J. K., & Treagust, D. F. (Eds.) (2009). *Multiple representations in chemical education*. New York: Springer.

Harrison, A. G., & Treagust, D. F. (1993). Teaching with analogies: A case study in Grade 10 optics. *Journal of Research in Science Teaching, 30*, 1291–1307.

Harrison, A. G., & Treagust, D. F. (1996). Secondary students' mental models of atoms and molecules: Implications for teaching chemistry. *Science Education, 80*, 509–534.

Posner, G. J., Strike, K. A., Hewson, P. W., & Gertzog, W. A. (1982). Accommodation of a scientific conception: Toward a theory of conceptual change. *Science Education, 66*, 211–227.

Treagust, D. F., Venville, G., & Harrison, A. (2001). Improving the effectiveness of using analogies in teaching and learning science. *SCIOS: The Journal of the Science Teachers' Association of Western Australia, 37*(1), 6–11.

Venville, G. J., & Treagust, D. F. (1998). Exploring conceptual change in genetics using a multidimensional interpretive framework. *Journal of Research in Science Teaching, 35*, 1031–1055.

PART II
IMPLEMENTING THE ART OF TEACHING SCIENCE

CHAPTER FOUR

TEACHING STRATEGIES FOR SCIENCE CLASSROOMS

Denis Goodrum and Amelia Druhan

OUTCOMES

By the end of this chapter you will be able to:

- Understand the issues of scientific literacy and student learning theory and their impact on teaching strategies
- Understand how to develop an inquiry-based approach to teaching
- Understand different student-centred models of teaching
- Understand how to structure lessons for meaningful learning
- Understand how to organise student teams and develop specific strategies for inquiry-based teaching
- Understand some of the benefits of working in a collaborative and supportive teaching team.

INTRODUCTION

The purpose of this chapter is to provide some simple and practical advice on how to improve the quality of teaching, which will result in better learning by your students. To understand the evolving development of teaching strategies, it helps to appreciate the influence of two significant forces that have emerged in recent years.

The first issue to consider is why science is taught in our schools. In previous years, the prevailing view was that school science was necessary for the initial preparation of scientists or science-related careers. Notwithstanding the importance of this consideration, today we generally believe that the purpose of teaching science in our schools is to promote scientific literacy. In simple terms, scientific literacy refers to the extent to which people are able to use science in their daily lives. This shift in focus has had a profound impact on what and how we teach.

The second major influence on teaching approaches revolves around our understanding of how people learn science. Chapters 2 and 3 have explained in detail the current ideas on learning and the factors that affect learning. While there is much we still do not know about learning, research over the past 50 years has shown the limitations of previous teaching practices. Our present views on learning provide some valuable insights into the types of teaching strategies we need to employ in order to provide opportunities that will result in more meaningful learning by students.

WHAT IS SCIENTIFIC LITERACY?

There is widespread agreement within the education and broader community that the purpose of science education is to develop scientific literacy. The authors of the national review of Australian science teaching and learning (Goodrum, Hackling & Rennie, 2001) define the attributes of a scientifically literate person, as shown in Figure 4.1.

These attributes inform the type of learning we expect from the compulsory years of schooling. For this learning, it is important for a teacher to be able to relate learning to a real-world context that is meaningful for the student. Obviously, students who seek occupations in science-related fields would pursue their interest in post-compulsory studies. All students, however, have the right to a science education that enables them to feel confident and able to deal with the scientific issues that impact on their lives.

If you believe in a science education that promotes the development of scientific literacy, then there are some expectations about the way science is taught. Many of these expectations are embedded in

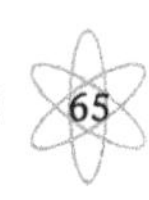

FIGURE 4.1: Attributes of scientifically literate people

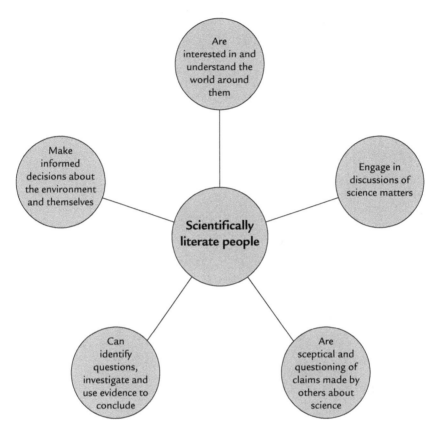

what is known as the inquiry-based approach. Snapshot 4.1 attempts to outline some of the changes required to teaching when there is a commitment to inquiry-based teaching.

In examining this snapshot, it would be wrong to suggest that one column contains only good teaching approaches and the other only poor approaches; rather, it is a question of emphasis. There is a need to do more of one and less of another if you are committed to inquiry-based teaching. For example, there should be less emphasis on memorising the names of scientific terms and more emphasis on learning broad concepts that can be applied to new situations. But there will still be some scientific terms that are useful for a student to know and apply.

SNAPSHOT 4.1: An outline of inquiry-based teaching

Inquiry-based teaching requires *less* emphasis on	Inquiry-based teaching requires *more* emphasis on
• Science being interesting for some students	• Science being interesting for all students
• Covering many science topics	• Studying a few fundamental concepts
• Theoretical, abstract topics	• Content that is meaningful to the students' experiences and interests
• Presenting science by talk, text and demonstration	• Guiding students in active, extended student inquiry
• Asking for recitation of knowledge	• Providing opportunities for discussion among students
• Individuals completing routine assignments	• Groups working cooperatively to investigate problems or issues
• Activities that demonstrate and verify science content	• Open-ended activities that investigate relevant science questions
• Memorising the names and definitions of scientific terms and facts	• Learning broader concepts that can be applied in new situations
• Learning science mainly from textbooks provided to students	• Learning science actively by seeking understanding from multiple sources of information, including books, the internet, media reports, discussion and hands-on investigations
• Assessing what is measured easily	• Assessing learning outcomes that are most valued
• Assessing recall of scientific terms and facts	• Assessing understanding and its application to new situations, and skills of investigation, data analysis and communication
• End-of-topic multiple-choice tests for grading and reporting	• Ongoing assessment of work and the provision of feedback that assists learning

HOW DO STUDENTS LEARN?

Our understanding of how students learn affects the way in which we teach. In the past, the transmission model of learning influenced teaching. In this model, it was believed that the mind of a student was empty and the role of the teacher was to fill it with scientific facts and principles. Teaching was acquainted with telling. This teacher-telling or didactic approach became entrenched in our school system, with a related content-based testing regime. Even today, some secondary school teachers are influenced by the simplicity of this approach, despite all we know about how students learn.

The prevailing view of learning, explained in previous chapters, is that people construct meaning from what they previously know and the new experiences or information they encounter. Learning is an active process. Learners make sense of their world by developing meaningful constructions between what they know and the new experiences that change what they know. Learning is therefore a continual incremental process of comparing, testing and adapting. To learn new ideas and skills takes time and varies with individuals. Taking all of this into account, the *Australian Curriculum: Science* (ACARA, 2012) emphasises an inquiry-based approach to teaching and learning. The inquiry-based approach reflects our understanding of how students learn, and outlines some important teaching principles that have a profound impact on the way teaching occurs (see Chapter 6 for more information about an inquiry-based approach to science teaching and learning).

Explore before explain!

Unfortunately, some teachers explain scientific ideas to students without providing a context or experiential base for the students. The impact of such explanations is minimal. For a scientific explanation to be effective, a teacher must first create or tap into experiences upon which the explanation is based. Such an approach has a stronger chance of providing meaning to the student. There are many ways in which teachers can provide experiences or help students relate to previous experiences. The most common is to provide hands-on activities that allow students the opportunity to inquire and investigate. For example, if a person is to develop an understanding of floating as a concept, they need to have experience with objects that float and those that sink, or with sinking objects that could be made to float. Through questioning, discussion and explanation, ideas associated with floating can be developed from the direct hands-on experiences of the student.

Recognising pre-instructional knowledge and experience

As we now know, all students come to any learning situation with some preconceived ideas. These ideas and experiences have an impact on how and what students learn. A teacher needs not only to appreciate what pre-instructional ideas are held by students, but to know how to build on this understanding.

There are a number of simple strategies a teacher can use to identify the ideas or experiences students have. One approach, at the beginning of a new topic, is to ask students to write a sentence or two (or draw a picture) to describe their initial understanding of the new concept. For example, in introducing a unit on energy, students could be asked to write a simple sentence containing the word energy and then answer the question 'What is energy?' Another approach is to pose a problem, perhaps using a picture as a stimulus. Students could discuss possible solutions as a class or in small groups. For example, Josh said he got his energy from sleeping but Amin said he got his from food. Who is right?

As a general principle, a teacher should always allow time to revise the previous lesson before starting a new lesson. This could be as simple as a quick three-question quiz to begin a lesson. Not only will this settle the class and prepare them for work, but students' responses will give insight into what they remember and understand from the previous lesson.

Ensuring student involvement

Students need to be interested and engaged if they are to learn. Good teachers continually attempt to spark curiosity by relating learning to current events or personal experiences. The experiences and events provide context and serve as 'hooks' on which students can hang new learning and ideas. For example, a recent television show might provide the basis for raising an issue related to the given topic. Creative teachers are effective in using popular activities and events to illustrate teaching ideas.

Hands-on activities enhance student understanding. For example, to understand the ideas of electrical current or voltage, teachers need to provide opportunities for students to play with batteries (dry cells) and light bulbs. The more personal the concrete involvement, the greater the potential for learning.

Encouraging student discussion

In previous years, it was believed by some that the quietness of a teacher's class was a measure of teaching quality. Today we realise that quietness does not necessarily correlate with learning. This does not diminish the importance of classroom management skills, but the significance of student discussion in facilitating learning is much more appreciated.

As students attempt to construct meaning and understanding, they need to test and verify their thoughts by discussing them with their peers and their teacher. By chatting about their ideas in small groups or as a class, students can refine and adjust the conceptual pictures they create in their minds. Ideas need to be related to evidence and views need to be justified.

This does not mean teacher explanation is not important. It is, but it needs to be used judiciously for maximum impact. In an effective classroom, there is a balance between teacher explanation and student discussion.

The other important skill a teacher needs to develop is the skill of summarising the ideas generated from student discussion in a coherent manner. A whiteboard summary of these ideas is a good way to provide worthwhile notes for students. In developing this summary a teacher can challenge and refine possible alternative conceptions or dispel inaccurate information.

Developing conceptual understanding

Intellectual rigour is an important issue in learning. Many science educators believe rigour is measured not by the number of scientific facts that are memorised but by the depth of conceptual understanding. There is a difference between learning for memorisation and learning for understanding. If you understand a concept, you can apply this understanding to a new situation. Many present-day curriculum documents outline learning outcomes in terms of developing levels of conceptual understanding rather than lists of science content to be covered.

Teaching for conceptual understanding is more challenging than the traditional view of teaching facts and principles. Despite the challenges, most teachers try to pursue the goal of more effective learning for their students. While one can simplistically classify learning into two categories–learning for memorisation and learning for understanding–the fact is that there are many shades of grey between these two ideas. Learning for understanding will entail being able to remember some factual information relevant to the particular concept. It is a question of emphasis, as explained earlier.

The role of questions and questioning

In traditional lessons, the driving force of teaching is teacher explanation. In inquiry-based teaching, the main engine for facilitating learning is the use of questions and discussion. Teachers need to develop an effective questioning technique to be successful.

To improve your questioning technique, use the following simple but powerful skills:

- *Ask a balance of broad and focused questions.* Broad questions like 'What do you observe about this flower?' and 'Why are the parts of a flower arranged as they are?' stimulate thinking among students. In traditional classes, narrow or closed questions usually dominate and are mainly used to challenge students to recall information. There are occasions in a discussion when there is value in the teacher focusing student thinking with a narrow question. Unfortunately, many teachers only ask narrow questions. In inquiry lessons, it is better to have a balance of questions that range between broad and narrow.
- *Allow for sufficient wait time.* Wait time is the time you, as a teacher, are willing to wait for students to answer a question. Research strongly indicates that if you allow three seconds or so, students will learn better. This time provides the opportunity for student reflection and comparison. If a student answers quickly, you should allow another three seconds. Hence students will be able to think further about the question. Remember that it is you, the teacher, who controls the wait time–not the students.
- *Use 'evaluation-free' responses.* To develop a better inquiry atmosphere in a class, it has been suggested that it is better to avoid comments like 'good boy', 'great answer' and 'well done'. Rather, responses are accepted or rejected on available evidence. By using an 'evaluation-free'

style of responding to students, a more normal discussion results. This approach encourages independent thought and inhibits the common classroom game called 'guessing what the teacher thinks'. In this game, praise is bestowed on students who are successful in reading the teacher's mind rather than thinking for themselves.
- *Listen.* A good teacher is a good listener. By listening to a student's response, you attempt to understand the thinking behind the answer and as a result can ask more thoughtful and effective follow-up questions.

A useful resource for learning more about questioning and opportunities for practice is the Science by Doing resource *Effective Questioning* (Australian Academy of Science, 2011a).

WHAT IS A USEFUL TEACHING MODEL?

To help translate the ideas about learning into classroom action, various authors have devised teaching/learning models that suggest how teachers can organise their science lessons effectively. These models tend to emphasise aspects of the previously described principles. While there is a similarity about the models, the differences reflect the varying degrees of emphasis on the principles. To illustrate, the 5E model is described here. This model is commonly used in Australia.

The 5E model

The 5E model (Bybee, 1997) is a simple model that is used in the primary science curriculum resource *Primary Connections* (Australian Academy of Science, 2005). It has been adapted for use in the secondary setting by the Science by Doing program (Australian Academy of Science, 2011b).

The 5E model consists of five distinct but interconnected phases.

1. *Engage.* The interest of students is captured through a stimulating activity or question. Students have the opportunity to express what they know about the unit topic or concept so that they can make connections between what they know and the new ideas being introduced.

2. *Explore*. Students explore problems or phenomena through hands-on activities, using their own language to discuss ideas. This exploration provides a common set of experiences that allows the new ideas to make sense.
3. *Explain*. After the engage and explore experiences, explanations and scientific terms are provided to students to help them develop their ideas.
4. *Elaborate*. Students apply what they have learned to new situations. They have discussions using the newly acquired language to clarify their understanding.
5. *Evaluate*. Students evaluate what they have learned and learning is assessed.

While this simple model works effectively in the primary setting, the case is different for secondary science. In secondary science, learning activities are often arranged better in a more cyclical way rather than the linear progression indicated here. For example, students may go through several cycles of Explore, Explain and Elaborate before moving on to Evaluate. This is due to the increased complexity of scientific concepts covered in the secondary years. Individual activities within a unit do not need to follow the whole sequence of the 5Es. Sometimes an activity focuses on one, although commonly more will be involved.

HOW MIGHT I BRING THESE IDEAS TO LIFE IN A CLASSROOM?

Structuring an inquiry-based lesson

One of the major ideas intrinsic to this chapter is that students learn more effectively from activity and experience rather than from listening to teacher explanation. These activities may involve hands-on inquiry, discussions and information research. Some teachers believe that in moving from teacher-centred to student-centred learning, the teacher has less of a role to play in the student activity. The opposite is true. The teacher in student-centred or inquiry-based learning needs to help to structure situations through which students can learn more effectively through questions and relevant comments.

All activities proceed through three simple phases:

1. Introduction
2. Activity
3. Conclusion

Within any lesson, this sequence may be repeated more than once.

1. Introduce the activity or investigation (brief)
   - Capture the interest of students by:
     - relating to personal experiences
     - asking provocative questions
     - relating to a previous lesson
     - using an engaging demonstration
     - relating to TV, film, or a recent event.
   - Outline the activity, explaining any necessary advanced organisation.
   - Explain equipment arrangements.
   - Outline time and outcome expectations.
2. Student activity (main time allocation)
   - Assist groups or individuals with materials and their activity.
   - Discuss ideas with groups and individuals, challenging them to think more deeply about what they are doing.
3. Conclude activity with discussion (adequate time needs to be allowed)
   - Students share results of activity.
   - Through questioning, help students summarise the main ideas.

It should be noted that the last phase is by far the most difficult, even for experienced teachers. Commonly, not enough time is allocated to this phase. Practice and planning are the keys to honing one's skills in concluding lessons effectively. Examples of activity lessons structured in this manner are provided in the Science by Doing resource *Inquiry-based Teaching* (Australian Academy of Science, 2011b).

Cooperative learning and group work

Working in a group or team enables students to share their experiences and to consider different points of view and solutions to a problem.

Cooperative learning is an approach that encourages students to work together to help them learn better. Teams develop the social skills of sharing leadership, communicating, building trust and managing conflict. These skills take time to develop but the longer-term benefits are worth the effort.

The benefits of cooperative learning include:

- *More effective learning.* Students learn more effectively when they work cooperatively than when they work individually or competitively. They have a better attitude towards their schoolwork.
- *Improved self-confidence.* All students tend to be more successful when working in groups, and this builds their self-confidence.
- *Better class management.* When students work in cooperative groups, they take more responsibility for managing the equipment and their behaviour.
- *Teaching students how to work cooperatively.* Even though in most classes there is a balance between individual, team and class activity, students still need to work together regularly to develop effective team learning skills.

Use the following ideas in planning cooperative learning with your class:

- Assign students to teams rather than allowing them to choose partners.
- Vary the composition of each team. Give students opportunities to work with others who might be of different ability levels, sex or cultural background.
- Allow sufficient time for each team to learn to work together successfully.
- If the number of students in your class cannot be divided into teams of equal numbers, form groups of smaller rather than larger sizes. It is more difficult for students to work together effectively in larger groups.
- Some research suggests that for lower secondary students a group size of four with a gender balance provides a better basis for co-operative learning.
- Consider the use of specific team jobs to help students work together in a team.

Team jobs

For classes—even lower secondary classes—that have limited experience in working in groups, there is value in considering the use of specific team jobs. Students are assigned jobs within their team. While each team member has a specific job, they are accountable for the performance of the team and should be able to explain the team results and how they were obtained. It is important to rotate team jobs each time a team works together, to give all students an opportunity to perform different roles. It has been suggested that colour coding (for example, coloured wool bracelets) could be used to distinguish team jobs.

The possible team jobs are:

- *Manager (red).* The manager is responsible for collecting and returning the team's equipment. The manager also tells the teacher if any equipment is damaged or broken. All team members are responsible for cleaning up after an activity and getting the equipment ready to return.
- *Speaker (blue).* The speaker is responsible for asking the teacher or another team's speaker for help. If the team cannot decide how to follow a procedure, the speaker is the only person who may seek help. The speaker shares any information obtained with team members. The teacher may speak with all team members, not just the speaker. The speaker is not the only person who reports to the class; each team member should be able to report on the team's results.
- *Director (green).* The director is responsible for making sure that the team understands the team activity and helps team members to focus on each step to be completed. When the team has finished, the director helps team members to check that they have completed all aspects of the activity successfully. The director provides guidance but is not the team leader.
- *Reports coordinator (yellow).* The reports coordinator is responsible for ensuring team members have completed all necessary reports, data collection and relevant worksheets. The coordinator is not necessarily the team reporter or recorder. All team members can be called upon to report on behalf of the team. The coordinator ensures that each member of the team has the necessary information so that they can report if required to the class.

Team skills

In addition to team roles that help teachers manage the work of small groups, it is important to help students develop skills that make teams more cohesive and improve learning. Teachers need to assess their students' team skills and focus on each skill that would enhance their work. The choice of skills will depend on the skill level of the particular class. Teachers need to name the skill they wish to develop, then explain to the class what is expected and how the skill will enhance students' group work and learning. In addition to this, teachers need to give regular feedback on students' use of the selected skills. It is better to focus on one skill at a time.

Students can be encouraged to apply the following skills to improve group management:

- Move into your groups quickly and quietly.
- Speak softly so only your team-mates can hear you.
- Stay with your group.

Students can be encouraged to apply the following skills to help groups function as a team:

- Use your team-mates' names.
- Look at the person speaking to you.
- Listen to others without interrupting.
- Praise others.
- Treat others politely.

Students can be encouraged to apply the following skills to enhance learning:

- Contribute ideas to the discussion.
- Encourage others to participate.
- Question the ideas of others, but disagree with the idea, not the person.
- Modify your ideas when provided with new information.

Support for embedding cooperative learning into your classroom practice can be found in the Science by Doing resource *Student Learning* (Australian Academy of Science, 2011c).

Specific teaching strategies

A range of different teaching strategies support the inquiry-based approach; these include collaborative and cooperative learning opportunities.

Concept mapping

Concept maps allow students to represent diagrammatically what they know about the links and relationships between concepts. They allow students to access prior knowledge and provide teachers with feedback on what is known or unknown and/or what is misunderstood, either at a single point or over time. Concept maps are designed to increase the student's ability to organise and represent thoughts and help with reading comprehension.

How it works. When concept maps are first introduced, model their use at the whole-class level. Brainstorm ideas as a class and ask students to assist jointly in grouping the words generated. Explain that each concept can be used only once. Link relationships with arrows or lines, and talk aloud to model the cognitive processes involved. Ask students to assist in identifying and labelling the relationships between concepts. Note these on the linking arrows or lines.

Example. When introducing the topic of energy, write the word 'energy' on the whiteboard with a box around it then ask 'What other ideas are related to energy?' Write these words on the whiteboard with each word in a box and a line connecting each word box. You may, for example, have the following words connected: energy–movement–direction–forces–friction–gravity. The resulting diagram will look like an asymmetrical spider web (see Figure 4.2). Students who have experience with concept mapping could be asked to prepare a personal concept map of energy at the start of the unit. Then ask them to repeat the exercise at the end of the unit. Students could compare their before and after ideas as outlined in the interactive model described earlier in the chapter.

Brainstorming

The purpose of brainstorming is to generate ideas quickly—it is a creative problem-solving strategy.

How it works. Quantity is more important that quality; all ideas are accepted and not criticised. Hitchhiking (building from each other's ideas) is encouraged. Write exactly what is said—no paraphrasing.

FIGURE 4.2: An example of a concept map on energy

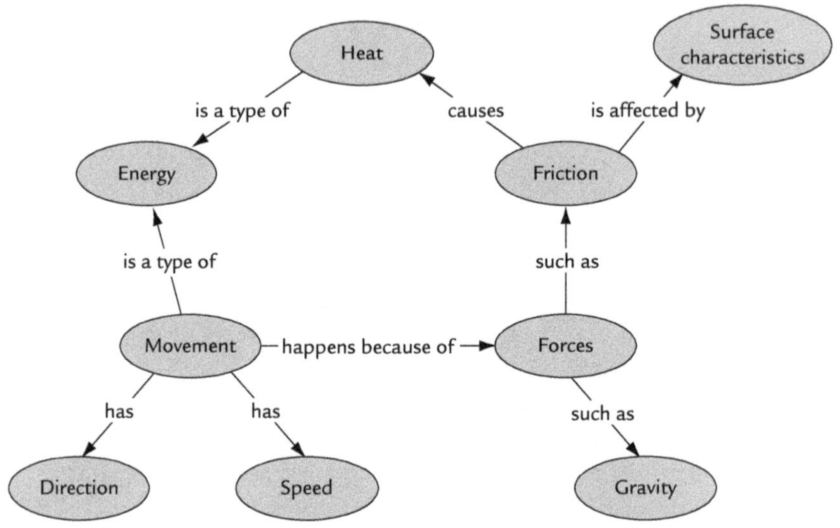

Example. At the start of any investigation, there is value in reflecting on the factors or variables that could impact on the investigation. Brainstorming could be used to do this. Write these ideas on the whiteboard as students call them out. Remember, you should not assess the worth of any suggestion until you have written up all suggestions.

Envoy

This strategy encourages students to learn from each other and take responsibility for learning. It helps students to develop listening and oral skills, and promotes skills in synthesising and summarising.

How it works. Students are formed into groups and are given a topic to discuss. One student from each group is selected to be the 'envoy'. When the group has completed its discussion of the topic, the envoy reports to another group and outlines what was discussed. The envoy also listens to a report from the group they are visiting. The envoy then returns to their original group, which has also received a report from another group's envoy, and they exchange new ideas. Each group should now have input from two other groups.

Example. Divide the class into groups of, say, four students and ask them to develop an explanation for why dinosaurs no longer exist.

After fifteen minutes of discussion, ask each group to select a person who will go to another group and describe the group's explanation. Use a circular approach for sending an envoy to the next group. In this way, no group will miss out. The envoy will return to their original group with reactions to the explanation.

Gallery walk

Student or group work is placed around the room and students are given the opportunity to view other students' work and to 'show off' their own.

How it works. Student work is placed around the room and students are given time to circulate and view the display. Students can use the opportunity to read information prepared by others or consider the way the information is presented. They can collect information from the work of others or peer-assess using a prepared set of guidelines.

Example. Divide students into groups of three and ask them to design a device for using the Sun to heat 200 mL of water. The students could draw their device on a large piece of paper. The drawings are then placed on tables and the class moves around, examining the designs.

Jigsaw

This strategy provides a structure for group work and also allows students to cover a broad amount of information in a shorter period of time.

How it works. Students are formed into 'home' groups of about five or six. The topic is divided up into sections and each student in the home group is given a different aspect of the topic to research. The home groups split up and the students form into 'expert' groups so all members in one group are researching the same aspect of the topic. Students research their aspect of the topic in the expert groups and prepare to report to their home group. Students return to their home group and take turns to report as the expert on their aspect of the topic.

Example. The class is divided into teams of five students who are asked to investigate types of energy. Each member of the team is assigned a type of energy to examine. Within the room, there have been established energy centres on particular energy types like 'chemical energy' or 'solar energy'. After each student has received their energy type, they go to the particular energy centre and find out as much as possible about that type by reading the available material, by searching reputable internet sites and/or by chatting with the students at that centre. The students then return to their original team and each member makes a presentation to their team on their chosen topic. They could also prepare a short handout for each member of the team.

Adopting inquiry-based strategies: The power of collaborative teaching teams

When asked, most experienced teachers will report that they have worked in a variety of teams and settings over the course of their careers. Of those experiences, many will say that the most rewarding were those involving a cohesive team of teachers with strong support for each other. This anecdotal evidence is supported by research indicating that student learning outcomes are improved when teams of teachers collaborate to plan lessons and units, develop and review assessment tasks, and reflect on their teaching (Hord & Sommers, 2008). Often, the term used to describe these teams is the professional learning community, or PLC.

What characterises a PLC? How is a PLC different from a team of teachers who enjoy each other's company, get along well and share drinks on a Friday afternoon? Research (DuFour, 2004) suggests that there are three key characteristics of an effective team of teachers, or PLC:

1. *A focus on student learning.* All teachers hold the belief that every student in their care has the capacity to learn.
2. *Time and support to work together.* The school values the opportunity for teams of teachers to meet regularly for planning and reflection.
3. *Initiatives are reviewed over time.* After implementation, the new ideas are reviewed to determine their effectiveness. Has it worked? How could we improve the strategy? Has it done what we wanted it to?

The Science by Doing project mentioned in this chapter holds the notion of a PLC at the heart of its professional learning approach. A case study from a Science by Doing school is the best way to illustrate the work of an effective teaching team. See Snapshot 4.2.

Why make mention of the power of teams here? In busy school life, there can be a strong pull to become self-sustaining—concerned only with what is happening in one's own classroom and with one's own students. Without ever intending to, teachers can easily come to be working *around* each other rather than *with* each other.

SNAPSHOT 4.2: An example of a professional learning community

At one Australian secondary school, the head of department asked her team of teachers if they were happy with the way they use questioning in their classrooms. With an inquiry-based Australian curriculum in the wings, was it time to consider whether their use of questioning could be improved? Her staff agreed that it was. Over the following week, the eight teachers worked in pairs to visit one another's classrooms for a ten-minute period. In that time, the observer recorded each question the teacher asked on a separate sticky note. In the following department meeting, all of the questions were collected. The teachers sorted them according to their degree of openness and the thinking skills required to answer them using Bloom's Taxonomy. They discovered that the vast majority of questions asked of students were closed, requiring simple recall of knowledge to answer. From this point, the teaching team developed a strategy to improve their questioning techniques, using the Science by Doing *Effective Questioning* professional learning resource to support them in their efforts. Most importantly, their strategy was punctuated with opportunities to review and gather data on their progress to ensure that their attempts were having the desired result.

Be on the lookout for opportunities to work collaboratively with your colleagues when implementing the teaching strategies from this chapter. Ensure the collaboration has a focus on student learning. Be realistic about your starting point and avoid trying too much too soon. While your efforts may be seen as yet another task in your busy professional life, in the long run working as part of a cohesive and supportive team makes for effective, satisfying and rewarding experiences. And the research shows that student learning is sure to benefit as a result.

Further information and resources to support the work of effective teams can be found at the Science by Doing website (<www.science.org.au/sciencebydoing>).

SUMMARY OF KEY POINTS

This chapter began with two questions that have a profound impact on teaching. Why do we teach science? And how do we learn science effectively? These questions led to the ideas of scientific literacy and constructivist learning, from which a series of teaching principles were implied and described. These principles were then embedded in a teaching model known as the 5E model. Using the principles, a suggested approach to planning lessons was outlined, with advice provided on how to develop cooperative learning using a team approach. The chapter concluded with a variety of specific strategies, including relevant examples. This chapter also provided information about how student learning outcomes may be enhanced when teachers work as part of a coordinated, collaborative team or professional learning community.

DISCUSSION QUESTIONS

4.1 What is scientific literacy and how does it influence science teaching?

4.2 How does the inquiry-based approach differ from the way you were taught science in school?

4.3 How might you use the 5E teaching model when planning a unit of work?

4.4 Describe three different lessons that utilise some of the inquiry-based strategies described in this chapter.

4.5 Describe three opportunities where you could collaborate with a colleague/colleagues to improve an aspect of your teaching practice.

REFERENCES

Australian Academy of Science (2005). *Primary connections.* Canberra: Australian Academy of Science. Retrieved 24 November 2011 from http://www.science.org.au/primaryconnections.

Australian Academy of Science (2011a). *Effective questioning: A stimulus for professional discussion.* Canberra: Australian Academy of Science. Retrieved 24 November 2011 from http://www.science.org.au/sciencebydoing.

Australian Academy of Science (2011b). *Inquiry-based teaching: A stimulus for professional discussion*. Canberra: Australian Academy of Science. Retrieved 24 November 2011 from http://www.science.org.au/sciencebydoing.

Australian Academy of Science (2011c). *Student learning: A stimulus for professional discussion*. Canberra: Australian Academy of Science. Retrieved 24 November 2011 from http://www.science.org.au/sciencebydoing.

Australian Curriculum, Assessment and Reporting Authority (ACARA) (2012). *The Australian Curriculum: Science*. Retrieved 24 November 2011 from http://www.australiancurriculum.edu.au/Science/Rationale.

Bybee, R. W. (1997). *Achieving scientific literacy: From purposes to practices*. Portsmouth, NH: Heinemann.

DuFour, R. (2004). What is a professional learning community? *Educational Leadership*, *1*: 1–6.

Goodrum, D., Hackling, M., & Rennie, L. (2001). *The status and quality of teaching and learning of science in Australian schools: A research report*. Canberra: Department of Education, Training and Youth Affairs.

Hord, S., & Sommers, W. (2008). *Leading professional learning communities: Voices from research and practice*. Thousand Oaks, CA: Corwin Press.

CHAPTER FIVE

PLANNING IN SECONDARY SCIENCE

Donna King

OUTCOMES

By the end of this chapter, you will be able to:

- Understand the benefits of planning in secondary science
- Design a science teaching program that uses constructivism as a referent
- Plan and prepare lessons that support a learner-centred approach to teaching and learning science

INTRODUCTION

Planning is an important part of learning to be a secondary science teacher. Effective planning requires teachers to design logical and coherent learning experiences that engage and challenge students. This chapter outlines methods of planning secondary science units and lessons based on a constructivist framework. While constructivism comprises a family of theories (see Chapter 2), they all have in common the centrality of the learner's activities in creating meaning.

In this chapter, constructivism will be used as a referent for planning teaching sequences that afford students opportunities to construct knowledge through both individual and group activities. Important steps in the planning process will be highlighted, such as the consideration of students' pre-instructional knowledge, recognition of the variety of teaching and learning strategies available and the inclusion of ongoing assessment.

Planning for teaching science in secondary schools requires three levels of consideration. First, at the macro-level, broader planning occurs at the whole-school level. Second, at the meso-level, unit plans are developed for a particular topic and year level; and third, at the micro-level, lesson planning occurs (Hudson, 2010). This chapter discusses these three levels, including examples or snapshots of teachers' planning documents to highlight the differences between the levels.

WHOLE-SCHOOL PLANNING

The first planning document that science teachers use in their schools is the science syllabus, which is the mandatory document devised by a government body associated with the relevant state or territory department of education. The syllabus provides teachers with a sequence of teaching and learning structures that are achievable for each age and stage of student development (Hudson, 2010). For example, in Queensland the Essential Learnings structure the science syllabus, providing teachers with a set of key learnings identifying what should be taught, and the important concepts students have opportunities to know, understand and be able to do (Queensland Studies Authority, 2008). Each state in Australia has a similar syllabus document, which are consistent with the *Australian Curriculum* (see Chapter 7). The *Australian Curriculum* is in the process of nationwide implementation and will provide the basis of planning, teaching and assessment for K–12 school science.

Science curriculum

The syllabus document is used by teachers for the first broad, or macro, level of planning where core science content applicable to specific student levels is obtained. The levels indicate progressions of increasing sophistication and complexity in learning outcomes (Queensland

School Curriculum Council, 1999). Once the syllabus documents have been scrutinised, a school science curriculum is planned. A science curriculum is a teacher's intended plan, including content, pedagogy, and assessment linked to achievement standards and school policies (Hudson, 2010). In larger secondary schools, it is often the responsibility of the head of science to coordinate the planning of the curriculum with the teachers for each year level.

The science curriculum or whole-school plan presents an overview of the school's approach to teaching science. Based on the syllabus document, the whole-school plan ensures all concepts are addressed and directs teachers to the topics and key ideas they will address when planning units of work. Generally, the whole-school plan is developed for specific year levels and incorporates the sequential development of science concepts from each of the various science knowledge areas (or strands) mandated by the syllabus. Snapshot 5.1 presents a section of the science curriculum plan for Year 8 from a secondary school in Queensland. The units designed for this school spanned approximately four to five weeks. At a glance, any teacher of Year 8 science can see the topics, strand and concepts they will include in their units of work and lesson plans.

SNAPSHOT 5.1: A section of a Year 8 whole-school curriculum plan

Unit name	Strand	Knowledge and understanding
Science is Matter	Natural and Processed Materials	• Changes of physical properties of substances can be explained using the particle model. • Matter can be classified according to its structure.
Cells and Systems	Life and Living	• Complex organisms depend on interacting body systems to meet their needs internally and with respect to their environment.

Unit name	Strand	Knowledge and understanding
Cells and Systems	Life and Living	• All the information required for life is the result of genetic information being passed from parent to offspring.
Energy to Burn	Energy and Change	• Energy can be transferred from one medium to another. • Energy is conserved when it is transferred or transformed.
Science is Forces	Energy and Change	• An unbalanced force acting on a body results in a change in motion. • Objects remain stationary or in constant motion under the influence of balanced forces.
What is a Reaction?	Natural and Processed Materials	• Changes in physical properties of substances can be explained using the particle model. • Matter can be classified according to its structure. • Chemical reactions can be described using words and balanced equations.

There are many aspects of a whole-school curriculum plan not included in Snapshot 5.1—for example, aims and rationale, specific objectives, school assessment policy and recommendations for catering for diverse learners. The school's context and culture, available resources and needs of the community must be considered when developing a science curriculum (see Chapter 7). Although schools are required to adhere to the prescribed syllabus, they have the freedom to choose their pedagogical approach and underlying theories of teaching and learning. While not every science teacher in the school may choose the same pedagogical approach, recent research in science education supports a learner-centred approach using constructivism as a referent. This requires teachers to view constructivism as a 'set of beliefs about knowledge and a set of reflective tools' that enable the science teacher to choose strategies and models that optimise students' learning of science (Tobin, Tippins & Gallard, 1995, p. 47). As a beginning teacher, the whole-school plan may already be developed, and once you have familiarised yourself with it you can begin your unit planning.

PLANNING UNITS OF WORK

A unit of work is a series of science lessons focused on the concepts in a topic outlined in the science curriculum. This is the 'middle picture' or meso-level for planning to teach science in secondary classrooms. Prior to planning the unit, the teacher needs to become familiar with the content, decide on the pedagogical approach that will underpin the learning experiences and identify opportunities for gathering information about the students' learning. To help teachers sequence the learning experiences, there are a number of teaching/learning models that can be used in the planning process. These models help teachers structure the lessons into phases and order activities appropriately. Chapter 4 described the 5E model that can be used for planning a sequence of teaching and learning activities. Models vary in the number of steps or phases utilised. Teachers generally choose the model that is most suitable for their approach to teaching and learning. Table 5.1 presents two more teaching models that prioritise a learner-centred approach to teaching science. A brief analysis of these two models and background information for each one is provided below.

These two models, like the 5E model, originate from a constructivist framework that acknowledges how students' cultural or everyday experiences influence their views about the world. Such a framework accepts that students' pre-instructional ideas may not be the same as

TABLE 5.1: A comparison of the steps in the Interactive Teaching Model and the Orientating, Enhancing, Synthesising Teaching Model

Interactive Teaching Model	Orientating, Enhancing, Synthesising Teaching Model
• *Preparation:* Teacher selects and researches topic.	
• *Before views:* Students' pre-instructional ideas are discussed.	• *Orientate:* Teacher introduces students to topic and elicits students' pre-instructional knowledge.
• *Exploration:* Students involved in topic through an exploratory activity.	
• *Students' questions:* Students are invited to ask questions about the topic. • *Investigation:* Teacher and students select questions to explore. Students construct knowledge through investigations.	• *Enhance:* Activities are designed and implemented that afford students opportunities to construct knowledge of key concepts.
• *After views:* Students' final views are compared to pre-instructional views.	• *Synthesise:* A blending of canonical science with the real world. New terms and concepts are consolidated and reinforced.
• *Reflection:* Establishment of what has been verified and what needs to be revisited.	

the scientific view, and as a result learning experiences in the classroom need to challenge these ideas. Therefore, like the 5E model, these two additional models consist of phases that elicit students' pre-instructional knowledge; engage students in activities where new science ideas may be constructed or pre-instructional ideas are challenged; and finally, allow students to reflect on their learning. This final stage of reflection affords students opportunities to verify new understandings and compare them with their initial views. While each model emphasises the construction of conceptual meaning by students, there are some differences between the models that are outlined below.

The Interactive Teaching Model, developed by Biddulph and Osborne (1984), can be represented by seven steps or phases where students are active participants in their learning. The approach encourages students to ask investigable questions that are answerable through specially designed exploratory activities. The teacher helps the students plan the investigations that address the questions. Students' pre-instructional views are compared with their final scientific ideas, revealing the learning that may have occurred.

The second model has three phases: orientating, enhancing and synthesising (Queensland School Curriculum Council, 1999). While the origin of this Orientating, Enhancing, Synthesising Teaching Model is unknown, it may have its roots in the three-step instructional sequence known as the learning cycle that was developed by Robert Karplus and colleagues in the 1960s. This three-phase approach is designed to orientate students to the problem or phenomenon to be explored; enhance students' understanding of the problem or phenomenon through investigations; and synthesise their learning through their demonstration of what they have learned. Some teachers prefer to use only three phases in the planning of interactive science units and lessons.

Although these two models have been shown as a linear sequence of steps, there may be to-ing and fro-ing between the various steps as teachers and students revisit stages to reinforce students' learning.

Flexibility and creativity can be incorporated in the stages or phases of the unit plan through innovative pedagogical approaches that provide a wide variety of learning experiences for students. Planning the unit affords teachers opportunities to choose innovative approaches to teaching science, such as context-based (a real-world context is central to the learning), problem-based (a problem to be solved structures the learning), project-based or inquiry-based science (a project or inquiry designed by the student structures the unit). Each of these approaches is further elaborated below.

Problem-based learning (PBL) focuses on a problem to be solved using an inquiry-based approach. For example, the problem may be:

> After the flooding in Brisbane in early 2011, the Brisbane River had a serious problem with water quality, requiring the council to closely

> monitor its health before allowing any recreational activity to resume. You are hired by the Brisbane City Council to write a report about the health of the Brisbane River. The report should include an analysis of water quality tests from which a recommendation is made about the suitability of the river for recreational use.

In such a way, the students are required to design an inquiry-based investigation that provides sufficient data to answer the problem that is posed. The teacher structures the unit of work around the problem, supporting students with the design of the inquiry, the experimental work and analysis of data.

Like PBL, project-based science (PBS) takes an investigative approach to the teaching and learning of science. Through a PBS approach, students design an inquiry that involves them finding the solution to a meaningful question, such as 'Which material is the best insulator' or 'How does the temperature of the water affect the dissolution of the sugar?' The timeframe for the project depends on the complexity of the question; however, unlike PBL, it does not have to be the focus of the whole unit of work. The project may be used to explore some of the key science concepts that structure the unit, which are mandated by syllabus documents. Many secondary schools incorporate PBS in science competitions where students design and carry out an investigation of their choice, culminating in the presentation of the results at a science fair.

A context-based approach is when the 'context' or 'application of the science to a real-world situation' is central to the teaching of the science. In such a way, the science concepts are taught on a 'need-to-know' basis—that is, when the students require the concepts to understand the real-world application further. While a context-based approach contains characteristics that are similar to PBL or PBS approaches, it is not identical to them. In context-based chemistry for example, students may be required to investigate a project such as the water quality of their local creek. Such projects are central to the context-based unit, link to students' real-worlds and may be student-driven to a significant degree. In these ways, a context-based approach shares similar characteristics with the PBL and PBS approaches. However, not all context-based approaches are centred on a driving question, problem or project. For example, the context could be 'the air we breathe' and students may complete a series of experiments on the different gases in the atmosphere, asking questions that require chemistry concepts to be taught to understand the context. In such a way, there is not one main investigation that structures the whole unit. Therefore, content taught on a 'need-to-know' basis could be taught as students ask questions about an inquiry or as they ask questions about the context as a result of individual experiments, their own reading or in-class discussions.

All three approaches—PBL, PBS and context-based—attempt to link science with students' everyday experiences by providing rich opportunities for students to make connections between canonical science and real-world phenomena. Effective teachers vary their teaching strategies and engage students in interesting and innovative advancements in science. For example, in Queensland the teachers of Year 12 chemistry in one school decided to create a new unit on nanoscience. The unit was entitled 'Materials: From Old to Nano'. The teachers researched the content through various websites and books, and designed an assessment task requiring students to apply nanotechnology and chemical principles to modify a chosen material used for a particular purpose, to enable it to become more useful to society. The students were required to describe standard chemistry of their original material as well as nanotechnology using the higher order thinking skills of invention and justification (see Chapter 10 for more information about higher order thinking skills). While this was a considerable amount of work for the teachers, they were rewarded with a unit that was thoroughly enjoyed by the students. One teacher described the unit in the following manner:

> Nanoscience certainly captured the interest and imagination of the students and I think they really appreciated being able to study 'science in the making' so to speak. There is a plethora of information on the internet—it is almost overwhelming. It was challenging and exciting to be a learner as well as a teacher throughout the unit.

The planning process

While there are a wide variety of ways to plan a unit, teachers generally begin with a list of objectives, specific outcomes or key concepts obtained from the syllabus document. The next step is to decide on a teaching/learning model that prioritises a learner-centred pedagogical approach. At this stage, teachers may choose an innovative pedagogical approach that requires a specific way to plan the unit. For example, a 'context-based' unit requires the learning to be contextualised around a real-world context. In such a way, teachers can combine the chosen model with new approaches that support their own philosophy for teaching and learning.

Snapshot 5.2 provides a unit plan for a Year 9 science class. The environmental science unit adopted a context-based approach to teaching science using the 5E model (see Chapter 4) to structure the teaching sequence. The unit required students to complete a teacher-guided inquiry that assessed the health of the local creek (Spring Creek). Students conducted water quality investigations, analysed primary and secondary data sources, and wrote a scientific report that could be communicated to the local community via local government authorities. The report included a summary of the data derived from the water tests, an evaluation of the water quality of Spring Creek based on scientific evidence and a summary of environmental issues affecting the water quality. On each visit to the creek, the groups rotated through each of the activities, which included the following: animal population study, plant study, soil sampling and drawing of a site map, water sampling and water testing or pollution study. Once the groups were organised and the tasks clarified, the teacher allowed the students to manage the data collection, analysis and write-up by adopting a student-centred approach. Throughout the unit, the context was central to all learning and content was taught as students required it to make sense of their data and observations. After the unit was completed, the teacher made the following comments about using a context-based approach:

> It was surprising to see how well the students responded to this approach. Particularly in terms of coming up with questions, topics, etc ... to develop the initial unit plan then their ability to construct testing/recording procedures for when they were down at the creek. My goal when allowing the students to develop the unit was that they would identify areas that they felt were important and I really feel that this was achieved. The sense of ownership and clear understanding of the context of the unit greatly helped the students to form strong links between what they learned in class and what they were observing/exploring while at the creek.

When planning a unit of work, teachers access a vast range of resources, including curriculum documents and support materials,

SNAPSHOT 5.2: A contextualised approach to the Year 9 science (ten-week) environmental unit plan: Monitoring the Health of Spring Creek

Objectives	Specific outcomes	Key concepts
• Promote greater interest and hence engagement in science via the use of a context-based approach • Provide students with scientific skills such as investigation skills • Promote ways of thinking that foster improved scientific literacy • Afford students opportunities to work collaboratively with their teacher to direct their own learning and develop their own course of work	Students will: • Understand factors that affect the environment and specific ecosystems • Evaluate and explain the effects of anthropogenic factors on water quality and ecological systems • Analyse and evaluate data to draw conclusions • Explain the relationships between adaptations/variations of organisms within a specific habitat	• Biotic and abiotic factors • Interactions—food webs/food chains • Roles in webs—for example, decomposers • Habitats • Populations and communities • Natural cycles • Human impacts on ecosystems, including historical land use • Responsible environmental decision-making • Adaptations • Changes in ecosystems • Water quality analysis

Breakdown of unit: Key questions

Water quality	Ecology	The environment
What is meant by the term 'water quality'?	How do you determine whether something is living?	What is an environment?
How can we determine the quality of water? (i.e. what tests can be done?)	Can the location in which the organism is living have an effect on the organism (and vice versa)?	What are some major types of environment?

Water quality	Ecology	The environment
What factors affect water quality?	Why are animals living in different habitats, not the same?	What are natural cycles and why are they important?
Are all sources of water (e.g. creeks, rivers, etc.) the same?	Is the number of organisms living in an area important?	Can the environment as a whole be affected by humans and/or the organisms living in them?
Can human activity affect the water quality of a creek?	Are all the organisms in a habitat in some way linked (or important) to each other?	

Assessment (summative)

Report on the water quality of Spring Creek including:

- Site map
- Glossary of key terms
- Data collection based on weekly creek visits
- Food web diagram of organisms identified at the creek
- Reflective entries
- Interpretation of data and summary of water quality

Phase 1: Engage

Students are introduced to the context. They are considered environmental scientists who have been appointed by Spring Creek Senior High School to monitor the health of Spring Creek. They will develop a 'road-map' (or mind-map) for the unit that will determine the direction they will follow for the completion of the task. This will be a teacher-facilitated, whole-class discussion with key questions serving as prompts to elicit prior knowledge.

Phase 2: Explore

Students will make their first visit to the creek, where they will record observations and formulate questions about the environment and the testing site (bridge near scout hall). Students will be afforded opportunities to use the water quality-analysis equipment. Questions generated from this visit will be addressed in the subsequent lesson in class, identifying what students don't know and what they need to know. The road-map will be revisited to allow students opportunities to add questions or ideas to further direct the unit.

Phase 3: Explain

Weekly visits to the creek will continue, during which students collect the data they need to complete the investigation and begin to determine the health of Spring Creek. When the students demonstrate a 'need to know', the teacher will guide their learning through appropriate student-centred learning activities—for example, laboratory activities on water quality testing will help students understand the water quality parameters used in the determination of the health of Spring Creek. Information will be accessed through web-based resources when appropriate.

Phase 4: Elaborate

Students apply the knowledge they have gained of the creek system throughout the unit to draw conclusions about the health of Spring Creek and its related ecology. The assessment item (final report) will provide direction for this phase, but will not be the major focus. Extension will be made from the work the students have completed on the creek to other creek/river environments with a focus on the possible impacts of human activities on those systems. An appreciation of human effects on environments may translate to larger scale (state, national and global) approaches to environmental and resource management, leading to improved scientific literacy.

Phase 5: Evaluate

Students reflect on their learning, and the new understandings and skills they have developed. Reflective entries in student learning logs are completed. Students are encouraged to reflect on how they can apply their knowledge to other areas of science, the school community and their daily lives.

Learning experiences

- Student-directed learning
- Group work
- Student research
- Practical (i.e. hands-on) investigation and experimentation
- Case study
- Whole-class and small-group discussion
- Problem-solving
- Reflective learning

multimedia resources such as YouTube and the internet, student textbooks, software and television, excursion sites, professional science teacher associations, colleagues' knowledge and previous science programs (Preston & Van Roy, 2007). With advances in multimedia, teachers can also create their own resources for use in the classroom. For example, in the unit presented in Snapshot 5.2, the teacher created a video, using a flipcam about the possible health issues of Spring Creek. In the short video, he adopted the role of a reporter investigating the health of the creek. Students were delighted with the video, which generated further student questions about the creek environment.

Planning a unit of work is rarely a straightforward process, and often requires teachers to revisit the objectives, key concepts and outcomes while reordering the lesson sequence and modifying the assessment. Good unit plans are working documents that evolve and change as teachers meet the emerging needs of their students throughout the unit. Annotations can be recorded on the unit plan throughout the course of the unit to record deviations from the actual and the planned unit (Preston & Van Roy, 2007). For example, in the environment unit above, bad weather occasionally interfered with planned creek visits, prompting the teacher to devise alternative activities. Also, students required opportunities to revisit creek activities to refine further their data and to consolidate their results. Overall, the aim of unit planning is to create interesting and engaging units that challenge students, adopt a learner-centred approach and link with students' real worlds.

LESSON PLANNING

Once the unit overview is written, the individual lesson plans can be created. This is an important step for beginning teachers, since it enables the timing, flow and sequence of activities to be planned. Similar to curriculum plans and unit plans, there are many ways of designing a lesson plan. Templates exist for pre-service and beginning teachers that provide a structure for planning. Generally, teachers modify an existing template to suit their individual needs and the requirements of the school policy.

The first step in lesson planning is to determine the intended outcome or achievement standard using the unit plan that was written from the current syllabus mandated by the state educational authority. Not all students will achieve the outcome or standard proposed in your lesson; therefore it is referred to as an 'intended' outcome (Hudson, 2010).

The second step is to determine the key scientific concept that will be explored in the lesson. This is generally presented in one or two simple sentences. Three examples are given below:

- There are three different states of matter (solid, liquid, gas).
- Forces are pushes, pulls and twists.
- The heart is a pump.

The key scientific concept states simply and clearly the one main scientific idea you intend students to learn from the lesson. Starting with one key concept enables beginning teachers to focus their planning. This is helpful when there is a plethora of resources available that can be distracting for the beginning teacher.

The third step requires a plan of the teaching and learning sequence through the design of learner-centred activities. This step allows a timeframe to be allocated to various parts of the lesson and the planning of necessary resources. It is important to plan the lesson so that it aligns with the teachers' and the school's philosophies of teaching and learning that underpin the curriculum document and the unit plan. Try to choose teaching and learning activities that enable students to construct their own knowledge. Research indicates that didactic or transmissive lessons, where the teacher imparts a large body of content to students—by talking or giving notes, for example—rarely changes students' pre-instructional views of science, causing students to emerge from a science unit with very different understandings than those intended by the teacher (Tytler, 2004). Choose an activity that directly relates to the learning outcome and key scientific concept(s). Consider the needs of diverse learners in your class by preparing specific strategies or activities for them. This may include modifying activities for students with special needs or researching the history of the local area to include Indigenous perspectives. The chosen activities for the lesson will also provide the basis of the ongoing assessment for your class.

Assessment is discussed in detail in Chapter 8; however, it is important to plan for ongoing assessment in each lesson. In broad terms, assessment is information about a student's learning (Hudson, 2010). Since assessment, outcomes, key concepts and the teaching-learning activities are all interrelated, planning the lesson involves a constant interplay between all of these aspects. The assessment strategies chosen will determine the students' involvement in the science activity and the work that has been produced. There are a wide variety of assessment strategies that are both formative (diagnostic analysis to improve teaching and learning) and summative (collecting data for making judgements). For example, in the Year 9 environmental science unit, the teacher used the final report for summative assessment; however, some formative assessment strategies included students' oral responses to questions, initiative to raise questions and debate information, selection and justification of investigation design, class/group interactions and a checklist of specific laboratory skills.

An example of a lesson plan from a Year 9 environmental science unit is presented in Snapshot 5.3. This example occurs in the 'Explain' phase of the 5E model in the unit plan, and represents one of the many styles for presenting a lesson plan.

SNAPSHOT 5.3: Year 9 environmental science lesson plan on food chains and food webs

<table>
<tr><td>Key Learning Area: Science</td><td>Lesson topic: Food Chains and Food Webs</td><td>Year 9</td><td>Essential Learning: In ecosystems, organisms interact with each other and their surroundings</td><td>Time: 45 minutes</td></tr>
<tr><td colspan="3">Learning outcomes strand: Life and Living
By the end of this lesson, it is expected that students will:
• Understand the interconnection of plants and animals in their local creek system
• Be able to construct food chains and food webs
Key concept(s): A food chain shows how each living thing gets its food. Interconnected food chains form a food web.</td><td colspan="2">Prior knowledge
• Consumers and producers (Year 8)
• Food webs and chains discussed at the creek while observing the interactions in the creek system.</td></tr>
</table>

Resources for students	**Resources for teachers**	**Safety**
• Journals, laptops	• Flipcam video of animals taken at the creek • Activity of food web in envelopes	• Laptops used safely—opened on clean desks.

Introduction (5 minutes): Students to brainstorm animals and plants they have seen at the three previous creek visits recorded in their journals. Teacher will record these on the interactive whiteboard. Teacher to ask students which animals may be eaten by other animals on the board and which animals may eat plants; links them using inspiration software.

Body (35 minutes): Teacher asks students to form groups and to decide which of the examples on the board are food chains and food webs. Following a whole-class discussion, a class definition of food chains and webs is recorded on the interactive whiteboard. Terms such as first-, second- and third-order consumers are discussed. Teacher shows a video recorded at the creek of animals and asks students to predict a food chain for each—for example, water glider insect, crow, carp, turtle, butterfly. Teacher discusses food chains and webs for a variety of animals and plants that are in the creek systems highlighted in the video. Students are split into groups and given a packet with a variety of animals found in creek systems. They are to design a food web, classifying the animals and plants found in the envelope as first-, second- or third-order consumers.

Conclusion (5 minutes): Whole-class discussion on the possible food webs that have been created. Teacher reiterates the key concepts learned through whole-class questioning. Teacher asks students to hand in their final food webs for formative assessment. Students are reminded to look for evidence of these food chains and webs at the next creek visit.

Assessment: Food web created by students, students' responses to questions and discussion, students' questions.

Evaluation: Did students achieve the intended outcome/s? What could be improved? How could I plan this better next time?

There are three stages to this lesson: an introduction, body and conclusion. In the introduction, students' prior knowledge is obtained. The body of the lesson involves an interactive activity where students work in groups. Finally, in the conclusion the teacher sums up the intended outcomes of the lesson. Effective teachers use a variety of teaching strategies in their lessons, which afford students opportunities to construct their own knowledge. In the lesson in Snapshot 5.3, the group activity consisted of students constructing food chains and webs while determining the consumer order. This is an example of an interactive activity that challenges and develops students' ideas. At the end of the lesson, the teacher can evaluate or reflect on students' learning by asking: Did students achieve the intended outcome/s? What could be improved? How could I plan this better next time?

Health and safety

Often science lessons involve laboratory work, requiring teachers to plan the health and safety aspects of the lesson very carefully. When constructing your lesson plan, always include the health and safety requirements for the lesson since your students' well-being must be your first priority. For example, in the Year 9 environmental science unit, the creek visits required the teacher to explain carefully the students' expected behaviour at the creek. They recorded the health and safety requirements in their journals prior to the first creek visit. These included:

- following the required path to the creek and walking carefully and quietly
- sensible behaviour at all times at the creek
- inform the teacher of any allergies
- don't drink the water
- stay in shallow water when wearing waders
- avoid bugs and spiders
- be mindful of the general public who may be at the creek walking dogs, etc.
- sun safety—wear a hat
- common sense—no chasey games, etc. . . . no throwing rocks
- listen to the teacher.

Health and safety are important considerations for lessons both inside and outside the classroom. Often science lessons involve laboratory activities that need to be prepared carefully. Think about the basic steps of the activity and record any potential hazards in the lesson plan. Check with a laboratory technician or an experienced teacher if in doubt about potential hazards. Allocate time for explaining the health and safety requirements to the students prior to the activity. As a beginning teacher, it is important to remember that your students' health and safety is part of your duty of care and legal responsibility.

SUMMARY OF KEY POINTS

Planning for the teaching of science in secondary schools requires three levels of planning: macro (whole-school planning); meso (unit planning); and micro (lesson planning). Teachers who adopt a learner-centred approach using constructivism as a referent plan to elicit students' pre-instructional knowledge, followed by the design of interactive activities that challenge and engage students in the learning of key concepts and concluding with a summary of what has been learned. Reflecting on whether students achieved the intended outcome/s is the last stage in effective planning. Some outcomes may need to be revisited in subsequent lessons.

A variety of teaching approaches are available to secondary science teachers that can be incorporated into lesson plans. Beginning teachers are encouraged to trial a range of approaches once they have an understanding of the learning needs of their students. Effective teachers continually improve their practice through their openness to new ideas, reflecting on their teaching approaches and implementing innovative strategies into their everyday planning. Thorough planning from the whole-school level through to the classroom level is essential for whole-school continuity and the sequential development of concepts in secondary science.

ACKNOWLEDGEMENT

The environmental science unit examples came from a Queensland University of Technology early career research grant used for a project conducted with a Year 9 science class and the teacher, Mr Evan Winner. The nanoscience example was from a Year 12 chemistry teacher in Queensland, Ms Carolyn Liddy. The Year 8 unit examples were

summarised from the units of work at Pimlico Senior High School in Queensland. Thank you to Dr Christine McDonald, who read earlier versions of this chapter and provided constructive feedback.

DISCUSSION QUESTIONS

5.1 What are the benefits of planning in secondary science?
5.2 What does it mean to use constructivism as a referent when planning secondary science lessons?
5.3 How do effective teachers improve their practice in secondary science classrooms?

REFERENCES

Biddulph, F., & Osborne, R. (Eds.) (1984). *Making sense of our world: An interactive teaching approach.* Hamilton, NZ: University of Waikato.

Hudson, P. (2010). *Hudson's guide for teaching primary science.* Brisbane: Australian Academy of English Studies.

Preston, C., & Van Roy, W. (2007). Planning to teach primary science. In V. Dawson & G. Venville (Eds.), *The art of teaching primary science* (pp. 87–107). Sydney: Allen & Unwin.

Queensland School Curriculum Council (QSCC) (1999). *Years 1–10 Science Sourcebook Guidelines (Part 5 of 8)*. Retrieved 24 November 2011 from https://www.qsa.qld.edu.au/downloads/early_middle/kla_sci_sbg_05.pdf.

Queensland Studies Authority (QSA) (2008). *Essential Learnings.* Retrieved 24 November 2011 from http://www.qsa.qld.edu.au/7297.html.

Tobin, K., Tippins, D., & Gallard, A. (1995). Research on instructional strategies for teaching science. In D. Gabel (Ed.), *Handbook of Research on Science Teaching and Learning* (pp. 45–93). New York: Macmillan.

Tytler, R. (2004). Constructivist views of teaching and learning. In V. Dawson & G. Venville (Eds.), *The art of teaching science* (pp. 18–33). Sydney: Allen & Unwin.

CHAPTER SIX
INQUIRY AND INVESTIGATION IN SCIENCE

Mark W. Hackling

OUTCOMES

By the end of this chapter you will be able to:

- Justify using an inquiry approach to science teaching and learning
- Distinguish between various forms of practical work in science and the learning outcomes that can be achieved through them
- Describe the processes of investigating, the types of variables and how these relate to the research question or hypothesis and to the design of a controlled experiment
- Select appropriate scaffolds to support students' work through the phases of an investigation and describe a suitable instructional model to teach investigation skills

INTRODUCTION

Scientific inquiry is driven by questions or hypotheses about natural phenomena. Inquiry is pursued through gathering and interpreting evidence and then testing and revising explanations for those phenomena through an interplay between data and theory. The explanations are then validated by peer review and publication. Inquiry-based science education is based on the premise that learners must be actively engaged in gathering and interpreting evidence and constructing meanings for themselves, which is consistent with the nature of scientific inquiry and social constructivist views about learning (Hackling, Smith & Murcia, 2010). In schools, inquiry is pursued through a variety of forms of investigation, including searches of information and practical work in the laboratory or field.

School science practical work can be used to help students achieve a number of learning outcomes, including getting a feel for natural phenomena; developing investigation skills and processes; providing a platform of experiences on which conceptual understandings can be built; and giving students a sense of the nature of science, and the excitement of inquiry and discovery. Different forms of practical work develop different learning outcomes, so it is important to use a range of practical experiences to develop the full range of outcomes.

Traditional 'recipe-style' laboratory exercises in which students follow the teacher's instructions to answer the teacher's question provide little opportunity for student ownership and agency, intellectual challenge or engagement. Even though students are hands on, they are often minds off. Investigations allow students to plan and conduct their own experiments within a context and boundaries set by the teacher. Investigations provide a more authentic experience of the nature of science and require students to be both hands on and minds on.

This chapter will address a number of questions related to practical work in science: Why should we use an inquiry approach to science education? What learning outcomes can be developed through practical work in science? What opportunities for learning are provided by different types of practical work? What processes are required to complete an investigation? How can student learning be scaffolded and facilitated?

INQUIRY-BASED SCIENCE EDUCATION

There are strong arguments from research that in order to maintain students' interest in the study of science, the curriculum needs to be more inquiry oriented and include more investigation work (Tytler et al., 2008). Moreover, science education should be inquiry based if we are to develop scientifically literate citizens and maintain students' interest in science. A working group of the Academy of Science has argued that inquiry-based science education supports students to develop inquiry skills and science understandings through their own activity and reasoning about evidence that they have gathered through their first-hand investigation of natural phenomena (Inter Academies Panel, 2006). This is consistent with the social constructivist view that students learn through their own activity and reasoning to develop meaning from experiences in conversation with others (see Chapter 2 for more about social constructivism).

The *Australian Curriculum: Science* is structured around three strands: science understandings; science as a human endeavour; and inquiry skills. These are said to be interrelated because the intention is that students will develop an understanding of science concepts and the nature of science through inquiry processes (ACARA, 2012; see Chapter 7). The centrality of inquiry is highlighted again in the aims of the curriculum, which include developing:

> an understanding of the nature of scientific inquiry and the ability to use a range of scientific inquiry methods, including questioning; planning and conducting experiments and *investigations* based on ethical principles; collecting and *analysing data*; *evaluating* results; and drawing critical, *evidence*-based *conclusions*. (ACARA, 2012, p. 1)

LEARNING FROM PRACTICAL WORK

There is an international consensus that the purpose of teaching and learning science in the compulsory years of schooling is the development of scientifically literate citizens. Scientifically literate citizens have the necessary knowledge and skills of science to enable them to function effectively in society. The attributes of scientifically literate people are discussed in more detail in Chapter 4 and presented in Figure 4.1. Practical work provides opportunities for students to develop learning outcomes that contribute to scientific literacy, including the skills and understandings needed to conduct scientific investigations and to critically evaluate the claims made by others based on scientific evidence.

Practical work also helps students develop a sense of the nature of science, which is an important component of the science as a human endeavour strand of the *Australian curriculum*. The nature of science refers to science as a way of knowing, or the values and beliefs inherent to scientific knowledge and its development (see Chapter 1). It is only when students practise as scientists, conducting their own investigations, that the nature of science becomes evident to them. An important characteristic of scientific knowledge is that it is evidence based. To be scientifically literate, students need not only an understanding of the big ideas of science (such as the nature of matter, evolution and energy), but also an understanding of the nature of scientific evidence (for example, accuracy and uncertainty). Students need opportunities to develop the understandings and skills associated with the collection, validation, representation and interpretation of evidence (Gott & Duggan, 1996). Students who understand the nature of scientific evidence should be able to detect when poor experimental design, control of variables or inappropriate sampling reduce the reliability of data, and when conclusions are not consistent with the data.

Students use science inquiry skills to plan and conduct investigations, organise and interpret data, reason with and critically evaluate scientific ideas and evidence, and communicate their findings. In summary, inquiry-oriented practical work provides opportunities for the development of inquiry skills, an understanding of the nature of science, and in particular an understanding of scientific evidence and the centrality of evidence-based drawing of conclusions for making credible knowledge claims in science.

TYPES OF PRACTICAL WORK

There are many different forms of practical work, including demonstrations, explorations, recipe-style exercises, investigations and projects. Practical work can be conducted in a range of contexts, such as the school laboratory, in the bush or at the beach, or at home.

Demonstrations are experiments performed by the teacher and observed by students that are used to model experimental methods and techniques, or to perform experiments that would be unsafe for students to perform themselves (such as demonstrating the burning of magnesium). As students play no part in manipulating the apparatus, they are not able to develop manipulative skills.

Explorations are unstructured mini-investigations where students have the opportunity to 'play' with materials and have concrete experiences of a phenomenon. Explorations are used to allow students to get a feel for phenomena such as magnetic attraction or crystallisation.

Most practical work conducted in secondary science takes the form of routine, recipe-style laboratory exercises in which students follow a procedure prescribed by the teacher to investigate a question set by the teacher (Hackling et al., 2001). Students follow the teacher's instructions to set up the prescribed equipment and make measurements and observations. Data interpretation is often structured by questions set by the teacher. For example, lower secondary students often conduct a laboratory exercise on the electrical conductivity of different materials in science. Upper secondary biology students conduct laboratory exercises on enzyme action and chemistry students conduct titration exercises. Exercises provide opportunities for students to practise experimental techniques associated with data collection and skills associated with data analysis and interpretation. There is no opportunity for students to develop skills associated with formulating a research question, identifying and manipulating variables or planning how to control variables.

Investigations require students to plan and conduct an experiment within the context and boundaries set by the teacher. As students are required to make decisions about the experimental design, data presentation and interpretation, there are opportunities for student agency, engagement and intellectual challenge, and to practise inquiry skills. Investigations are more inquiry oriented than exercises, and provide a more authentic experience of the nature of science compared with closed recipe-style laboratory exercises. Inquiry-oriented practical work has been shown to produce higher order learning outcomes than traditional closed, recipe-style laboratory exercises (Minner, Levy & Century, 2010).

Projects are a more extended form of inquiry, often involving a review of existing knowledge, investigation of several independent variables and reporting of findings to stakeholders. Projects often extend over several weeks, as they involve extensive fieldwork, observations or several experiments. For example, Year 9 students might conduct an extended project on wind turbines where they do background research about the efficiency and effectiveness of the power generation, survey local residents about health fears with regard to the turbines and conduct experiments to determine the noise levels produced by the turbines in comparison with other noise in the environment, such as highways.

Teachers should use a range of types of practical work so that students have opportunities to learn a wide range of understandings and skills. To improve the curriculum in secondary science, many of the laboratory exercises should be replaced with investigations so that students can learn how to plan their own experiments. The easiest way to do this is to simply remove the detailed procedural instructions from some of the exercises to open them up and turn them into investigations. For example, lower secondary students could be required to plan their own investigation on the electrical conductivity of different materials rather than being given a 'recipe' about how to do this.

Students need to build a foundation of skills, understandings and confidence before attempting more complex investigations and projects. Figure 6.1 illustrates an instructional sequence that prepares students for these more demanding tasks.

FIGURE 6.1: A learning sequence that prepares students for more complex forms of practical work in science

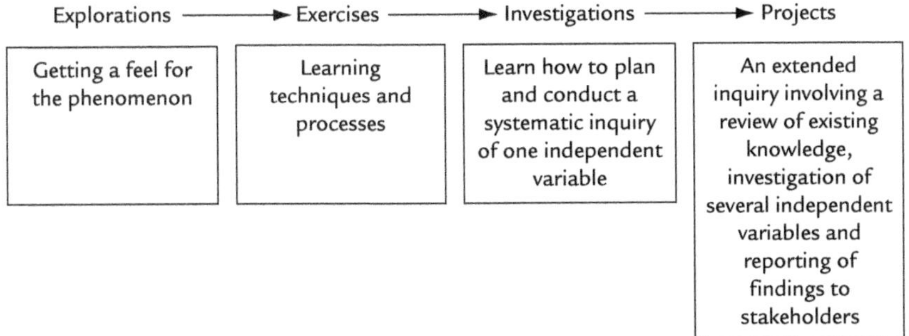

INVESTIGATING

There are many types of investigation; however, most investigations require students to *plan* the experiment, *conduct* the experiment and collect data, *process* the data and communicate findings, and finally reflect on their investigation, *evaluating* the quality of the findings and the investigation methods used. The evaluation phase focuses students on what they have learned from the investigation, and this can be carried forward to improve planning of the next investigation. Figure 6.2 illustrates a model of the investigation processes. In practice, these processes may not take place in the strict order of planning-conducting-processing-evaluating, as part-way through conducting

FIGURE 6.2: A model of science investigation processes

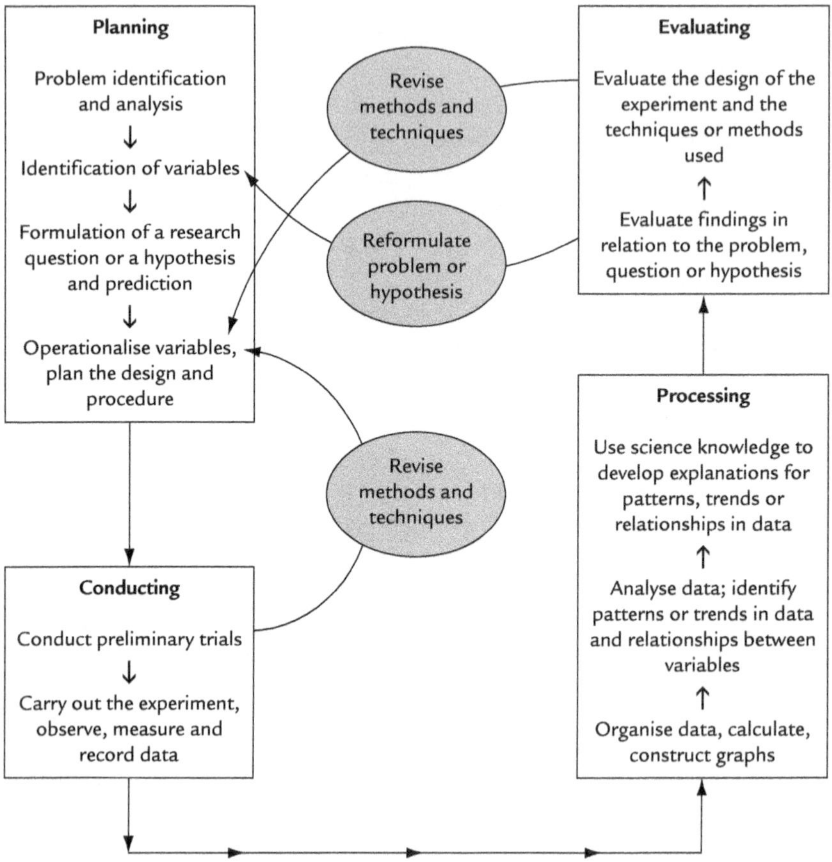

Planning

Problem identification and analysis
↓
Identification of variables
↓
Formulation of a research question or a hypothesis and prediction
↓
Operationalise variables, plan the design and procedure

Revise methods and techniques

Reformulate problem or hypothesis

Revise methods and techniques

Evaluating

Evaluate the design of the experiment and the techniques or methods used
↑
Evaluate findings in relation to the problem, question or hypothesis

Conducting

Conduct preliminary trials
↓
Carry out the experiment, observe, measure and record data

Processing

Use science knowledge to develop explanations for patterns, trends or relationships in data
↑
Analyse data; identify patterns or trends in data and relationships between variables
↑
Organise data, calculate, construct graphs

(Hackling & Fairbrother, 1996).

the investigation, students may realise that further planning is required to improve the measurement technique or design of the experiment.

In addition to these four phases of investigation, there are opportunities for students to communicate their findings using posters, formal written reports and oral reports, and thereby practise communicating using scientific genres of reporting. The findings from investigations may also guide students' decision-making and actions in their own lives, and develop outcomes associated with acting responsibly (such as an investigation of air temperatures inside cars parked in the sun to help students realise the dangers of leaving pets in cars on hot days).

Implementing investigation work in science

Many teachers who have not previously implemented investigations with their students often raise concerns about doing this type of practical work. The most commonly cited concerns are listed below, with a response to each concern.

- *Investigations take longer to complete than laboratory exercises.* Many investigations do take longer to complete than exercises as time is needed for planning the experiment. Teachers should replace several exercises with a smaller number of investigations. In this way, practical work can be contained within the available time.
- *Students experience difficulty planning their own experiments.* Students who have not previously completed investigations will not have had the opportunity to learn planning skills. Teacher modelling and coaching, as well as explicit teaching of some skills, will be required.
- *Students will all want to do different experiments and it will be impossible to provide the equipment they require.* Teachers can easily limit students to the same investigation or to one or two independent variables for a given investigation, or limit them to using only apparatus that is supplied. As confidence increases, the teacher may open up the range of possibilities and allow students to place an order for equipment that will be brought to the next lesson.
- *Students will have accidents.* Teachers should require students to have their plan checked before they are permitted to carry out their investigation. It is also prudent to allow student access only to equipment and reagents that pose few safety concerns.

SCAFFOLDING AND FACILITATING STUDENT LEARNING

Investigations are unstructured problem-solving tasks that require students to take the initiative to devise an appropriate approach to the problem, experimental design and techniques. Many students need considerable support if they are to engage successfully in these tasks. Support can be provided by breaking the task into a series of steps and by modelling some of the more difficult inquiry skills.

Investigation planning and report sheets

Planning and report sheets guide students through a sequence of decision-making steps providing structure and scaffolding to support students while giving them responsibility for the decision-making. These scaffolds are structured by a sequence of questions and prompts. One scaffold, suitable for Year 6–10 students, is illustrated in Snapshot 6.1.

SNAPSHOT 6.1: Questions used to scaffold investigations for lower secondary science students

Question or prompt	Instructional purpose of the question or prompt
What question or hypothesis are you going to investigate?	Students focus on the problem and formulate a question or hypothesis for investigation.
What do you think will happen? Explain why.	Students make a prediction and justify their prediction—this activates pre-instructional knowledge for the investigation.
Which variables are you going to: • change • measure • keep the same?	Students identify and operationalise the key variables.
How will you make it a fair test?	Students reflect on their plan and ensure that variables are controlled.
What equipment will you need?	Students think about the apparatus they will require to conduct the investigation.
Describe your experimental set-up using a labelled diagram, and explain how you will collect your data.	The plan is set out in detail using a diagram and the steps in their procedure.

(cont.)

Question or prompt	Instructional purpose of the question or prompt
Did you carry out any preliminary trials of your procedure to see whether your planned method of data collection would work? Were there any problems? What changes did you make to fix the problems?	These questions provide an opportunity for students to demonstrate that they conducted preliminary trials and have refined their procedure based on what they learned from the trials.
What happened? Describe your observations and record your results.	This prompts students to record their measurements and/or observations.
Can your results be presented as a graph?	This prompts students to decide whether it would be worth graphing their data.
What do your results tell you? Are there any relationships, patterns or trends in your results?	These questions prompt students to search for patterns in the data.
Can you explain the relationships, patterns or trends in your results? Use some science ideas to help explain what happened.	These questions prompt students to explain the patterns in their data using science concepts.
What did you find out about the question you investigated? Write your conclusion. Was the outcome different from your prediction? Explain.	These questions prompt students to summarise their findings as a conclusion and to compare their finding with their prediction. Discrepancies often occur between predictions and findings due to students' pre-instructional knowledge. Such discrepancies may cause students to reflect on their beliefs.

(cont.)

Question or prompt	Instructional purpose of the question or prompt
What difficulties did you experience in doing this investigation?	This question prompts students to reflect on the processes used in the investigation and identify difficulties experienced.
How could you improve this investigation—for example, fairness, accuracy?	This question helps students focus on what they have learned about improving their investigation processes.

Scaffolds such as the one illustrated in Snapshot 6.1 lead students through the investigation process and elicit from them information about their thinking and what they are doing at each stage of the investigation. Scaffolds therefore provide support to students, and the written record of the investigation provides information needed by teachers to assess students' investigation work. A number of planning and report sheets suitable for scaffolding primary, lower secondary and upper secondary students' investigations can be downloaded in electronic form (Hackling, 2005).

Operationalising variables

To understand the design of controlled experiments, students need to understand the three types of variable and the relationships between them. This is best explained in the context of an investigation of the effect of drop height on the bounce height of a tennis ball. The height to which a ball bounces depends on the height from which it is dropped. The bounce height is therefore the *dependent variable* (DV) and the drop height is the *independent variable* (IV). There are a number of other variables that could also possibly influence the bounce height, such as the surface on which the ball bounces, the ball type and the ball temperature. These other variables therefore need to be controlled (kept the same) so that we are sure that any change in bounce height is caused by the changes made to the drop

FIGURE 6.3: Relationships between independent, dependent and controlled variables

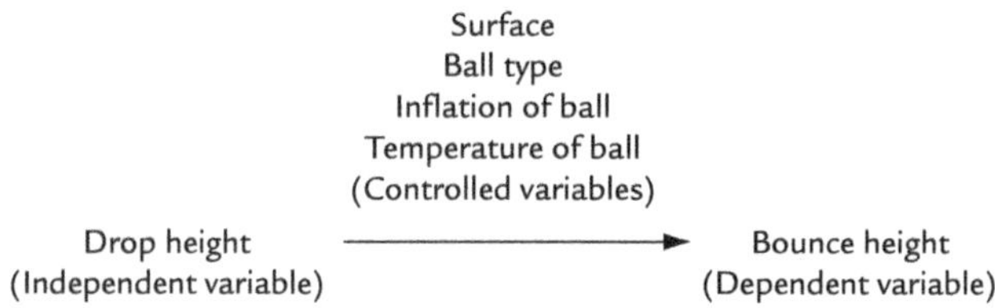

height rather than changes in the surface or ball. These relationships are illustrated in Figure 6.3.

One way of helping students understand the relationships between variables in a controlled experiment is to use a variables table. An example of a variables table is provided in Figure 6.4. Variables tables can be completed on an interactive or regular whiteboard using questioning to elicit the variables from students. In this way, the process of designing a controlled experiment can be modelled for students.

FIGURE 6.4: An example of a variables table

Research question: How does the amount of light affect the growth of seedlings?

What I will keep the same	What I will change	What I will measure
Type of seeds *Type of soil* *Amount of water* *Amount of fertiliser* *Size of container* *Planting depth of seeds*	*Amount of light:* • *dark* • *partial shade* • *full sun*	*Height of the seedlings*
Controlled variables	Independent variable	Dependent variable

In summary, in a controlled experiment, the independent variable is changed to see what effect it has on the dependent variable while all other variables that could potentially affect the dependent variable are kept the same.

Writing research questions and hypotheses

Many students experience difficulty in writing testable research questions and hypotheses. Students need plenty of experience working with research questions before they are introduced to hypotheses. Research questions are written in the form of a question about the possible relationship between an independent variable and a dependent variable. They can be written in a standard form that can be structured using the following algorithms:

What happens to ____________ when we change ____________ ?
(DV) (IV)

For example:
What happens to the *growth of wheat seedlings* when we change *the saltiness of the water*?

or

What effect does ____________ have on ____________ ?
(IV) (DV)

For example:
What effect does the *saltiness of water* have on the *growth of seedlings*?

Hypotheses are tentative declarative statements about the relationship between an independent variable and a dependent variable. They have a more complex structure than research questions. Hypotheses can be written in the following form:

This change to the independent variable
+ will cause this to happen to
+ the dependent variable.

For example:
Increasing the salinity of water (IV) will reduce (relationship) the growth of wheat plants (DV).

As many secondary science students have a focus on 'getting the right answer' in their practical work, which comes from extensive experience of closed laboratory exercises, hypotheses cause problems for many students when their data do not support their hypothesis. Students will often fudge their data to match the hypothesis to give the appearance of getting the right answer. Students have been shown

to commit this form of scientific fraud as they do not understand that the hypothesis may be wrong, or that there may be error associated with their data due to measurement error, poor control of variables, or small and unrepresentative samples. To write an hypothesis assumes that students have some knowledge about the phenomenon and the relationships between the associated variables. Hypotheses are therefore better suited to older, more experienced and more able students. Most investigations can be conducted successfully using research questions.

The cognitive apprenticeship model of instruction

It is helpful to conceptualise the teacher's and the students' roles in learning the complex skills of science as being analogous to that of the tradesperson and apprentice. The cognitive apprenticeship model of instruction (Hennessy, 1993) has as its main elements modelling, scaffolding, coaching, articulation and fading:

- The teacher *models* strategies for the students, making explicit their problem-solving processes (for example, models the process of plotting a line graph).
- The teacher provides *scaffolding* to structure the work of the students (for example, uses planning and report sheets to guide students through the steps of an investigation).
- The teacher works alongside students, *coaching* them on specific skills and strategies (for example, providing feedback and guidance on the measurement technique being used).
- Students are encouraged to discuss and reflect on their decision-making and strategies; *articulation* of tacit knowledge helps make it explicit (for example, students work in small groups so they can discuss their methods of controlling variables).
- As students gain competence, some of the scaffolding is *faded* away (for example, the planning and report sheets are withdrawn).

Types of investigation

In the same way that there are different types of practical work, there are also different types of investigation. Each type of investigation has a different variable structure and provides different opportunities for learning. This is illustrated with examples in Table 6.1.

TABLE 6.1: Examples and features of various types of investigation

Type of investigation	Example	Features
1. Testing types of materials	Which kind of paper towel holds most water?	Types or brands of materials are tested for absorbency, strength, stickiness, durability, etc. The independent variable is always discrete. Tests need to be repeated to give an indication of the extent of measurement and sampling error.
2. Investigating a relationship between two variables where repeat trials can be used	Effect of the height from which a ball is released on the height to which it bounces	Repeat trials and averaging are used because tests are non-destructive and the repeat trials give an indication of the extent of measurement error.
3. Investigating a relationship between two variables where replication can be used	What effect does temperature have on germination/dissolving?	Replication involves using several duplicate experiments set up at the same time. Replication is used because tests are destructive and can't be repeated, and the material or population may be non-uniform; hence replication gives an indication of the extent of sampling error.
4. Investigating the effect of several independent variables on one dependent variable	How do number of coils, length and thickness of wire, type of metal from which wire is made	There is a need to test a number of independent variables separately or in combinations on one dependent variable and

(cont.)

Type of investigation	Example	Features
often associated with a design problem.	and current affect the effectiveness of a heating element? How do you make a powerful heating element?	then develop a design brief.
5. Survey-type research where populations are sampled to investigate the relationship between two variables.	What is the relationship between height and arm span?	The population being tested is non-uniform and samples are selected based on the parameters being investigated. Sampling is randomised to control for interfering variables.

Type 1 investigations are very common in primary science as the independent variables are discrete (that is, in categories) and data are presented using bar graphs. Type 2 investigations are common in secondary science, as is the use of continuous independent variables (that is, data are continuous on a measurement scale such as length or mass) and representing data using line graphs. It is important to include a range of investigation types in the curriculum so that students are exposed to repeat trials, replication, discrete and continuous variables, bar and line graphing.

One of the most useful sources of science investigation ideas is the CSIRO's CREativity in Science and Technology (CREST) website. The CSIRO has a program of awards that can be earned by students for completing science investigations. The CREST website offers a list of suggested investigations at three levels (bronze, silver and gold) which students may wish to do individually as projects (see <www.csiro.au/org.CREST>). Science talent search competitions run by Australian state science teachers' associations provide wonderful opportunities and motivation for students to engage with investigation and project work in science (see <www.asta.edu.au>).

SUMMARY OF KEY POINTS

Practical work is an essential component of science programs for school students. It is through inquiry and investigation that science tests ideas and generates new knowledge. By conducting investigations and practising as scientists, students can get a sense of the nature of science, and learn skills and understandings at the heart of scientific literacy. Inquiry-oriented and investigative science programs actively engage students in learning, increasing their interest in science and developing those inquiry skills linked to reasoning with scientific processes, ideas and evidence.

DISCUSSION QUESTIONS

6.1 How would you justify to a colleague your decision to include more investigations in your teaching program at the expense of covering content?

6.2 What factors would you consider in planning a sequence of types of practical work and types of investigations to maximise learning outcomes?

6.3 Design a science investigation task that will engage students in authentic investigation in a real-world context. Your investigation should develop important inquiry skills and provide a platform of experience on which one of the fundamental concepts of science can be developed.

REFERENCES

Australian Curriculum, Assessment and Reporting Authority (ACARA) (2012). *The Australian Curriculum: Science.* Retrieved 24 November 2011 from http://www.australiancurriculum.edu.au/Science/Rationale.

Gott, R., & Duggan, S. (1996). Practical work: Its role in the understanding of evidence in science. *International Journal of Science Education*, *18*(7), 791–806.

Hackling, M. W. (2005). *Working scientifically: Implementing and assessing open investigation work in science* (rev. ed.). Perth: Department of Education and Training. Retrieved 24 November 2011 from http://www.eddept.wa.edu.au/science/Teach/workingscientificallyrevised.pdf.

Hackling, M. W., & Fairbrother, R. W. (1996). Helping students to do open investigations in science. *Australian Science Teachers Journal*, *42*(4), 26–32.

Hackling, M. W., Goodrum, D., & Rennie, L. (2001). The state of science in Australian secondary schools. *Australian Science Teachers Journal*, *47*(4), 6–17.

Hackling, M., Smith, P., & Murcia, K. (2010). Talking science: Developing a discourse of inquiry. *Teaching Science*, *56*(1), 17–22.

Hennessy, S. (1993). Situated cognition and cognitive apprenticeship: Implications for classroom learning. *Studies in Science Education*, *22*, 1–41.

Inter Academies Panel (2006). Report of the Working Group on International Collaboration in the Evaluation of Inquiry-based Science Education (IBSE) Programs. Retrieved 24 November 2011 from http://www.interacademies.net/File.aspx?id=7078.

Minner, D. D., Levy, A. J., & Century, J. (2010). Inquiry-based science instruction—What is it and does it matter? Results from a research synthesis years 1984 to 2002. *Journal of Research in Science Teaching*, *47*(4), 474–496.

Tytler, R., Osborne, J., Williams, G., Tytler, K., & Cripps-Clarke, J. (2008). *Opening up pathways: Engagement in STEM across the primary–secondary school transition*. Retrieved 24 November 2011 from http://www.deewr.gov.au/Skills/Resources/Documents/OpenPathinSciTechMathEnginPrimSecSchTrans.pdf.

CHAPTER SEVEN
THE AUSTRALIAN SCIENCE CURRICULUM

Vaille Dawson and Grady Venville

OUTCOMES

By the end of this chapter you will be able to:

- Argue the importance of school science education in Australia
- Appreciate the purpose of science curriculum documents
- Explain the rationale, scope and sequence of the *Australian Curriculum: Science*
- Differentiate an integrated curriculum from a discipline-based curriculum

INTRODUCTION

A quality education in science is a crucial outcome of schooling. All young people need a deep understanding of how the practice of science enables humans to make sense of the world around them. The knowledge produced by science allows us to solve problems and make informed, evidence-based judgements to improve our lives and those of others. For example, our understanding of science allows

us to develop drugs to treat diseases, build telescopes to search the furthermost reaches of the Universe, predict weather patterns and explain why certain chemicals react with each other in predictable ways. Many of the global problems facing humanity (such as climate change, food and energy shortages) require science- and technology-based solutions.

There are two key purposes of school science education in Australia. The first is to provide future scientists with a firm grounding in scientific concepts, skills and attitudes so that they have the background to continue with science study beyond the compulsory years of schooling. The second, and arguably the most important, purpose is to develop scientific literacy in all young people. Rennie, Goodrum and Hackling (2001, p. 494) state that:

> Scientifically literate persons are interested in and understand the world around them, are sceptical and questioning of claims made by others about scientific matters. They participate in the discourses of and about science, identify questions, investigate and draw evidence-based conclusions, and make informed decisions about the environment and their own health and well-being.

Over the past two decades, internationally and nationally, the quality of school science education has been severely criticised for its failure to both prepare future scientists and to produce a scientifically literate society (e.g. Osborne & Dillon, 2008; Tytler, 2007). As stated succinctly by Russell Tytler (2007, p. 1), 'science education in Australia, as in other post-industrial countries, is in a state of crisis'. In the developed world, including Australia, a smaller proportion of students are electing to study school science beyond Year 10. In the years up to Year 10, science is perceived to be boring and irrelevant. A decision to discontinue with science in Year 10 usually prevents students from pursuing future tertiary study and careers in science and engineering, and severely limits their opportunities to develop scientific literacy.

Since the mid-1970s, there has been a steady decline in the proportion of Australian students studying science (especially physics and chemistry) in the senior years of schooling (Lyons & Quinn, 2010). The reasons for the decline in enrolments are complex, and are due in part to greater subject choice and a greater proportion of young people staying at school. However, Lyons and Quinn identify three reasons related to science education. First, many young people do not view themselves as scientists. Second, science subjects are perceived to be more difficult and of less use than other subjects. And third, science fails to engage many students. If this trend in decreasing enrolments is to be halted or reversed, it is essential that science teachers provide students with a challenging, engaging and relevant science education.

Despite the decreasing proportion of students continuing with science, Australian students perform very well in international studies of scientific literacy. For example, the Programme for International Student Assessment (PISA), coordinated by the Organisation for Economic Cooperation and Development (OECD), found that in the 2006 tests, out of the 57 participating countries Australian 15-year-old students were outperformed in the domain of scientific literacy by only three countries (Finland, Hong Kong–China and Canada) (Thomson & De Bortoli, 2008). In 2009, Australian students achieved similar average scores to those in 2006 but were outperformed by six of the 65 participating countries (Thomson et al., 2010).

In PISA 2006, students' attitudes to science and environmental issues were also measured. Of concern is the fact that, despite the outstanding results in scientific literacy, Australia was ranked 54th of 57 countries on an index indicating students' general interest in studying science (Thomson & De Bortoli, 2008). Moreover, Australian students scored lower than the OECD average in relation to how concerned they were about the environment (ranked 46th of 57 countries) and how optimistic they were that environmental problems can be solved (ranked 47th of 57 countries). If we consider that our young people will need to tackle environmental (and other) issues, then it is crucial that the school science curriculum includes the necessary understandings, skills and values, and is also delivered in an engaging and inclusive way. (See Chapter 9 on motivation and Chapter 12 on equity.)

WHAT IS CURRICULUM?

The type of learning offered to students is dictated through curriculum documents. Before considering Australian science curriculum documents, the term 'curriculum' is defined and explained. A simple definition coined by Decker Walker, Emeritus Professor of Education at Harvard University, is that 'the curriculum refers to the *content* and *purpose* of an educational program together with their *organisation*' (Walker, 1990, p. 5). The *content* of a curriculum refers to the components or topics. In science, there typically are knowledge and understanding aspects (for example, physics, chemistry, biology, earth science and astronomy concepts), process skills (for example, posing questions, collecting and analysing data, constructing arguments) and affective factors (for example, valuing living organisms and scepticism). The *purpose* of the curriculum refers to the aims or objectives, and is usually linked to an over-arching goal of preparing the next generation of young people to achieve their full potential, live fulfilling lives and participate fully in society. The *organisation* refers to the structure (that is, simple to complex understandings), scope (breadth of content) and sequence (order and timing of content). The purpose, organisation and content of the Australian curriculum in science will be described in detail later in this chapter.

There are different forms of curriculum, depending on the audience (Van Den Akker, 1998). For example, there is the *ideal* curriculum (underlying philosophy of the curriculum), the *formal* curriculum (mandated curriculum documents or frameworks), the *perceived* curriculum (curriculum as interpreted by teachers), the *enacted* curriculum (the teaching strategies used by teachers in the classroom), the *experiential* curriculum (learning activities experienced by students) and finally the *attained* curriculum (the actual learning by the students). Alignment across these various levels of curriculum is not always evident, as the things that students actually learn can be quite different from the ideal curriculum. It is important for teachers to keep this factor in mind, as teachers are the key people responsible for interpreting and enacting the curriculum.

USING SCIENCE CURRICULUM DOCUMENTS

When you commence your first job as a beginning teacher, a question uppermost in your mind is likely to be, 'What do I actually have to teach these students?'

In some schools—especially larger ones—there may be well-documented teaching programs that set out a sequence of teaching and learning activities. Other schools may have nothing. However, it can be difficult to pick up another teacher's program and use it without understanding why particular outcomes, learning activities or assessments are specified. It is a bit like following a knitting pattern without having a picture of the whole garment. Who knows what the final product will look like? You need to be aware of what your students might already know and what they will need to know by the time they leave you. The most important source of information about *what* to teach and *how* and *why* will be formal curriculum documents.

Formal curriculum documents are provided to teachers by government educational jurisdictions to help them to know *what* to teach and *how* and *why*. These documents may be supported by a syllabus that prescribes in greater detail what is taught. The curriculum documents help teachers to plan teaching programs and lessons, select curriculum resources, develop learning activities and assess students' learning. Science curriculum documents provide information about the sequence, breadth and depth of science learning at each year level. Typically, scientific concepts are revisited throughout the years of schooling so that students are exposed to similar concepts at increasing levels of complexity as they progress. Although the terminology varies, the content areas of biology, chemistry, physics, and earth and space science, and the process areas of laboratory skills, scientific inquiry, nature of science and the role of science in society are generally included in formal curriculum documents.

The *experiential* curriculum (that is, the learning activities in which students participate) depends not only on the *formal* curriculum, but a number of other factors, including:

- curriculum support documents provided by the education sector (government, Catholic and independent)
- curriculum resources (laboratory equipment, science garden, animals) available at the school
- ICT resources and support (interactive whiteboards, data loggers)
- technical support (laboratory technicians)
- the priority given to science compared with other curriculum areas in your school and state/territory
- time allocation (single periods, block time)
- the financial budget allocated to science in the school
- teacher background, experience, expertise and interest
- teacher beliefs about how science should be taught
- student factors such as achievement levels, aspirations, previous science experiences and attitudes to science
- community and parental expectations.

AN HISTORICAL PERSPECTIVE

The Australian education system recently underwent a major change, with a shift from state and territory mandated curriculum documents to a new Australian curriculum. New Australian curriculum documents have been released in the learning areas of science, mathematics, English and history for kindergarten to Year 10. Before describing the Australian curriculum in science, it is useful to consider the recent history of science education in Australia.

In 1989, the Australian Education Council, which comprised the state, territory and federal education ministers, commissioned the development of national statements and profiles for eight broad curriculum areas, one of which was science. This led to the publication of *A Statement on Science for Australian Schools* (Curriculum Corporation, 1994a) and *Science—A Curriculum Profile for Australian Schools* (Curriculum Corporation, 1994b). The *National Science Statement* and *Profile* provided a framework for curriculum development. The science learning area was divided into four content strands: Life and Living; Natural and Processed Materials; Energy and Change; and Earth and Beyond. A fifth process strand was called Working Scientifically.

These curriculum documents were underpinned by a social constructivist and student-centred approach to teaching and learning. They moved away from a rigid syllabus style to a more flexible approach that would cater for students of varying science achievement levels and aspirations. It was recognised that students progressed at different rates so, rather than specify concepts according to age or year group, eight levels of achievement that reflected student learning were described. The term 'learning outcomes' was proposed so that the emphasis moved away from what the teacher taught to what the students would actually know, understand, do and value as a result of participating in the curriculum.

However, when the state and territory education ministers met with their federal counterpart to consider the *National Science Statement* and *Profile*, each of the six states and two territories decided to develop its own formal curriculum and support documents. In 2008, the state and territory education ministers and their federal counterpart released the *Melbourne Declaration on Educational Goals for Young Australians* (MCEETYA, 2008). Two goals were identified. They were:

1. Australian schooling promotes equity and excellence.
2. All young Australians become:
    - successful learners
    - confident and creative individuals
    - active and informed citizens.

The action plan to achieve these two goals stated that 'State, Territory and Commonwealth governments will work together with sectors to ensure world-class curriculum in Australia' (2008, p. 13).

The development of the new curriculum has involved Australia-wide consultation with practising science educators at the primary, secondary and tertiary levels, parents, industry groups, professional associations, community groups and other stakeholders. The findings of contemporary educational research on teaching, learning and assessment in science were considered. It was recognised that learning is an ongoing and active process, that students construct their own knowledge and that pre-instructional knowledge and experiences will influence student learning (see Chapter 2 for a discussion on how children learn).

In 2008, a 'shape' paper was released, followed by a 'framing' paper. These papers laid out a framework for science and were subject to broad, prolonged and rigorous critique. The Australian science curriculum documents are still undergoing a process of consultation and review, and are likely to change. Implementation in schools is planned to occur from 2012 onwards, with some variation across states and territories. The breadth and sequence of the Australian curriculum in science aligns with current (soon to be phased out) state and territory curriculum documents.

THE *AUSTRALIAN CURRICULUM: SCIENCE*

The *Australian Curriculum: Science* document is available in both a pdf and a hyperlinked web-based version (<www.australiancurriculum.edu.au>). The web-based version allows users to search according to their needs. A website user guide outlines how to navigate through the online documents. Using Walker's (1990) definition of curriculum, the purpose, organisation and content of the Australian science curriculum are summarised below.

Purpose

The *Australian Curriculum: Science* describes the rationale and aims of school science education from Kindergarten (the year prior to commencing Year 1, known by various names in different states and territories) to Year 12. In the rationale, science is described as a 'dynamic, collaborative and creative human endeavour arising from our desire to make sense of our world through exploring the unknown, investigating universal mysteries, making predictions and solving problems' (ACARA, 2012, p. 1). Arising from this definition, there are seven aims of the science curriculum. They are:

1. an interest in science
2. an understanding that science explains the living and non-living world
3. an understanding of scientific inquiry
4. an ability to communicate scientifically to a range of audiences
5. an ability to solve problems and make informed evidence-based decisions
6. an understanding of historical and cultural contributions to science
7. a knowledge base in biological, chemical, physics, earth and space sciences.

Organisation

The curriculum is organised into three interrelated *strands* (Science Understanding, Science as a Human Endeavour and Science Inquiry Skills), which are further divided into *sub-strands*. The sub-strands are described for each year of schooling. In addition, there are six *over-arching ideas* that are fundamental to science:

1. patterns, order and organisation
2. form and function
3. stability and change
4. scale and measurement
5. matter and energy
6. systems

Across all learning areas of the *Australian Curriculum: Science*, there are broad skills and behaviours that are considered important for all young people to achieve. These skills and behaviours are called *general capabilities*, and are embedded in the content of all curriculum areas. The general capabilities are:

1. literacy
2. numeracy
3. ICT competence
4. critical and creative thinking
5. ethical behaviour
6. personal and social competence
7. intercultural understanding

Finally, there are three *cross-curriculum priorities* that need to be included in all learning areas, including science. The cross curriculum priorities are:

1. Aboriginal and Torres Strait Islander histories and cultures
2. sustainability
3. Asia and Australia's engagement with Asia.

Content

Kindergarten to Year 10

The science curriculum from Kindergarten to Year 10 comprises three interrelated strands of Science Understanding, Science as a Human Endeavour and Science Inquiry Skills. Each strand is further divided into sub-strands. For example, in Years 7 to 10, Science Understanding is divided into sub-strands of biology, chemistry, physics, and earth and space science. Table 7.1 summarises the strands and sub-strands in the Australian science curriculum.

For each year level from Kindergarten to Year 10, there is a *year-level description*, a *year achievement standard* and a small number of annotated *work samples*. There are also *content descriptions* for each of the sub-strands. Although these terms initially may seem to be confusing, they are used consistently throughout the curriculum documents, and users will become familiar through regular use.

Years 11 and 12

In Years 11 and 12, there are four science subjects: biology, chemistry, physics, and earth and environmental science. At the time of writing,

TABLE 7.1: Strands and sub-strands in the *Australian Curriculum: Science*

	Strands		
	Science understanding	**Science as a human endeavour**	**Science inquiry skills**
Sub-strands	Biological sciences	Nature and development of science	Questioning and predicting
	Chemical sciences	Use and influence of science	Planning and conducting
	Earth and space sciences		Processing and analysing data and information
	Physical sciences		Evaluating
			Communicating

the content of these subjects is still under development. The content of each subject aligns closely with the current senior secondary subjects of chemistry, physics and biology, which are offered in all states and territories, and earth and environmental science, which is offered in Western Australia and New South Wales. Each of the subjects is divided into four units (one per semester across the two years) and the content is organised under the three strands.

CURRICULUM INTEGRATION

Almost all curriculum documents in the world, like the *Australian Curriculum*, are structured around subjects such as science, history, mathematics and English. As a consequence, the majority of secondary schools also are structured into departments based on these subjects, with subject-qualified teachers. This sometimes results in the enacted school curriculum being strongly compartmentalised, and students may not be able to see the big picture and connections between what they are studying and the real world. This is not ideal from an educational perspective because there is growing recognition that the major problems and issues that face humanity and the world in which we live, such as global warming and over-population, are not confined within the boundaries of the disciplines. They are cross-disciplinary problems, and in order to solve them we need to think and work from multiple disciplinary perspectives and in multi-disciplinary teams. Understanding and decision-making with regard to these problems is an important part of schooling because today's students are the citizens and decision-makers of the future.

The *Australian Curriculum* refers to cross-curriculum priorities, including sustainability, and strongly encourages teachers to integrate the three strands of Science Understanding, Science as a Human Endeavour and Science Inquiry Skills (ACARA, 2012). The *Australian Curriculum* also encourages science teachers to develop links to other learning areas including English, mathematics and history.

Integrated approaches to teaching science are essential to engage students in real-world issues of relevance to their lives and to enable them to understand complex, multi-layered concepts and problems that are often at the cutting edge of scientific research. For example, Elizabeth Blackburn, the Australian winner of the Nobel Prize for discoveries in molecular biology in 2009, led a multi-disciplinary research team that provided better understanding of the relationship between chronic stress, ageing and cancer (Trounson, 2010). Blackburn said that each of the scientists with whom she collaborated had deep knowledge of their respective field, and the collaborative process of the research boosted the outcomes of the project.

Another example is the 2010 Scopus Young Researcher of the Year in the Life Sciences and Biological Sciences category, University of Adelaide mathematical ecology researcher Corey Bradshaw. One aspect of Bradshaw's work was the development of a computer model to test scenarios in a virtual Kakadu National Park (located in the Northern Territory) to establish the cheapest and best culling programs to limit the damage from pests such as feral buffalo, horses and pigs (Conservation Gains a Technical Solution, 2010). Bradshaw said to *The Australian* newspaper's Higher Education Supplement: 'I realised the best thing I could do for my career was to get adept at mathematics' (2010). He further explained that 'mathematics is a fundamental component of all biology now, especially ecology, because it's such complex systems we're dealing with' (2010, p. 24).

Examples of integrated curricula

So what does an integrated curriculum look like? One secondary school in Perth offered an integrated project on solar boats to its academically talented Year 8 science class. The students studied science, mathematics and technology separately, but the three teachers of these subjects collaborated to allow the students to work in teams to design, build and test a solar boat. In science, the students learned about electrical circuits, solar energy and buoyancy. In mathematics they learned how to statistically analyse the trials they conducted with the components of their boats. The students also learned about time management and about angles of incidence so that they could work out the best angle for their solar panels on the day of testing. In technology, the students learned about materials and designs for fast boats. The term-long project culminated with an exciting race of all solar-powered boats. Not only did the students learn important concepts and skills in each of the subjects, they also learned about teamwork, and how teams function to produce technological products based on scientific knowledge.

Another secondary school in Sydney focused on a lake that was in the school's neighbourhood. A development of a new resort with a nine-hole golf course had been proposed to the local council and had caused considerable debate in the community. Students in the Year 9 class were given the opportunity to carry out research on different aspects of the proposed development. One group of students investigated a mosquito-like insect that used the lake as a breeding ground and the possible impact of the development on the life-cycle of the insect. Another group investigated the effect of fertilisers on lake water and the impact that fertilising and irrigating the golf course might have on the quality of the lake water and the species in the lake. Another group of students found out about the needs of a local boating club, including access to the lake and space for water skiing. Yet another group investigated the importance of the lake to the cultural and physical well-being of the Indigenous people living in the area. The project ended with a highly successful mini-conference where the findings of each of the various projects were reported as oral presentations and posters to fellow students, teachers, parents and invited community members.

Due to the highly discipline-based structures of curriculum documents, testing regimes and secondary school departments, integrated teaching and learning is challenging for teachers. These examples illustrate, however, that it is possible to break down the highly discipline-based boundaries that have built up around school subjects and that the benefits for students are worth the effort. Research has shown that high-quality integrated curricula for students of the twenty-first century include a significant degree of balance between disciplinary and integrated knowledge and considerable connection between local and global knowledge (Rennie, Venville & Wallace, 2012).

SUMMARY OF KEY POINTS

This chapter has described some of the key problems in science education and argued that a quality curriculum is essential to develop the next generation of scientists and to ensure all Australians have a high level of scientific literacy. The purpose, organisation and structure of a curriculum were discussed, and details of the new Australian science curriculum were described. Although the *Australian Curriculum* documents initially may seem daunting, support is available from education sectors, professional associations and other teachers.

DISCUSSION QUESTIONS

7.1 Visit the website of the *Australian Curriculum* (<www.australiancurriculum.edu.au>). Select a year level, strand, sub-strand and science content description. Identify three learning activities that you could use in teaching this part of the curriculum.

7.2 Consider an integrated curriculum focusing on sustainable houses, to be taught in Year 9 science. What discipline-based knowledge or concepts could be taught in such a unit? How could this knowledge be connected with issues on a global scale?

REFERENCES

Australian Curriculum Assessment and Reporting Authority (ACARA) (2012). *The Australian Curriculum: Science.* Retrieved 24 November 2011 from http://www.australiancurriculum.edu.au.

Conservation gains a technical solution (2010, 3 March). *The Australian Higher Education Supplement*, p. 24.

Curriculum Corporation (1994a). *A statement on science for Australian schools*. Melbourne: Author.

Curriculum Corporation (1994b). *Science—a curriculum profile for Australian schools*. Melbourne: Author.

Lyons, T., & Quinn, F. (2010). *Choosing science: Understanding the declines in senior high school science enrolments*. Research report to the Australian Science Teachers' Association. Armidale, NSW: University of New England. Retrieved 24 November 2011 from http://une.edu.au/simerr.

Ministerial Council on Education, Employment, Training and Youth Affairs (MCEETYA) (2008). *Melbourne Declaration on Educational Goals for Young Australians*. Melbourne: Author.

Osborne, J., & Dillon, J. (2008). *Science education in Europe: Critical reflections*. A report to the Nuffield Foundation. London: King's College London.

Rennie, L., Goodrum, D., & Hackling, M. (2001). Science teaching and learning in Australian schools: Results of a national study. *Research in Science Education, 31*, 455–498.

Rennie, L., Venville, G., & Wallace, J. (2012). *Knowledge that counts in a global community: Exploring the contribution of integrated curriculum*. London: Routledge.

Thomson, S., & De Bortoli, L. (2008). *Exploring scientific literacy: How Australia measures up. The PISA 2006 survey of students' scientific, reading and mathematical literacy skills*. Melbourne: ACER Press.

Thomson, S., De Bortoli, L., Nicholas, M., Hillan, K., & Buckley, S. (2010). *PISA in brief: Highlights from the full Australian report, Challenges for Australian education: Results from PISA 2009*. Melbourne: ACER Press.

Trounson, A. (2010, 24 February). Deep specialization key to collaboration. *The Australian Higher Education Supplement*, p. 23.

Tytler, R. (2007). *Re-imagining science education: Engaging students in science for Australia's future*. Melbourne: ACER Press. Retrieved 24 November 2011 from http://www.acer.edu.au.

Van Den Akker, J. (1998). The science curriculum: Between ideals and outcomes. In B. J. Fraser & K. Tobin (Eds.), *International handbook of science education* (pp. 421–447). Dordrecht: Kluwer.

Walker, D. (1990). *Fundamentals of curriculum*. San Diego, CA: Harcourt Brace Jovanovich.

CHAPTER EIGHT
ASSESSMENT OF AND FOR LEARNING IN SCIENCE

Mark W. Hackling

OUTCOMES

By the end of this chapter you will be able to:

- Explain the relationships between teaching, learning and assessment
- Distinguish between diagnostic, formative and summative forms of assessment
- Describe the characteristics of quality assessment items and tasks

INTRODUCTION

Assessment is the process of gathering and interpreting information about the progress of students' learning. Assessment has a powerful influence over what is taught and learned in science, as both teachers and students work towards assessments—especially end-of-topic tests. If assessments focus on recall of factual information, teachers will rush through lots of content and students will attempt to memorise that content, which results in superficial surface-level learning. If assessments focus on applying conceptual understandings and skills to

make sense of issues in the lives of students, they are more likely to attempt to learn for understanding, resulting in deeper learning.

Traditional assessment that focuses on mastery of factual information is the most powerful barrier to the reform of teaching so that it is more student centred, inquiry oriented and focused on developing scientific literacy. To reform teaching, we first need to reform assessment so that it rewards teachers and students who work towards the learning outcomes that contribute to scientific literacy.

The national review entitled *The Status and Quality of Teaching and Learning of Science in Australian Schools* (Goodrum, Hackling & Rennie, 2001) notes two important concerns about current assessment practice in secondary science: first, the over-emphasis on assessment of learning and the under-utilisation of assessment to improve learning; and second, the widespread use of traditional testing that focuses on the extent to which students memorise and recall science facts—this focus hinders the development of both meaningful understanding and outcomes that contribute to scientific literacy.

This chapter will address a number of questions related to assessment. What are the relationships between teaching, learning and assessment? What should be assessed? Why do we assess? How should we assess? What are the characteristics of quality assessment items and tasks? How is students' work marked and how are grades allocated?

WHAT ARE THE RELATIONSHIPS BETWEEN TEACHING, LEARNING AND ASSESSMENT?

Those who hold behaviourist, transmission model-based views about teaching and learning believe that the role of the teacher is to be the source of knowledge. According to this view, knowledge is transmitted through exposition and by giving notes for students to memorise. In this model, the purpose of assessment is to ascertain the extent to which the transmitted knowledge has been remembered, and this information is used to grade students and report to parents. This model is illustrated in Figure 8.1.

Contemporary constructivist learning theory helps us understand the powerful influence that existing conceptions—particularly alternative conceptions—have on students' construction of meaning and their learning from classroom activities (see Chapter 2). Hattie's (2009) analysis of research that determines the influence of various factors on

FIGURE 8.1: A behaviourist view of the relationships between teaching, learning and assessment

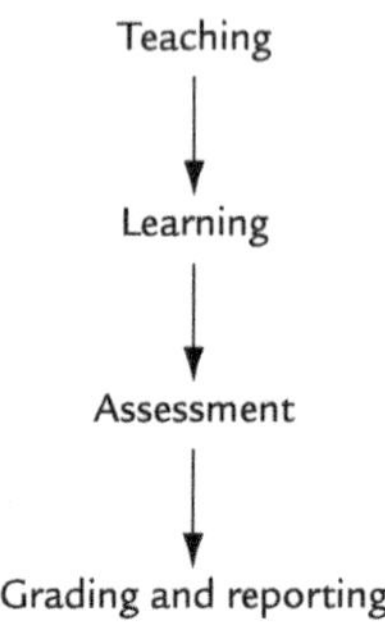

students' achievement shows that students' pre-instructional knowledge is the factor that has the greatest influence on learning outcomes. Consequently, assessment strategies that reveal students' existing conceptions early in the instructional sequence have been included in a number of constructivist-based teaching-learning models. Assessment before and during the instructional sequence can provide information to teachers and students that can be used to improve teaching and learning. Of all the strategies that teachers use, monitoring students' learning and providing them with feedback is the one that has the greatest influence on their achievement (Hattie, 2009). In a constructivist model, the relationships between teaching, learning and assessment are less linear, and more complex and interactive, compared with that in a behaviourist model. Figure 8.2 provides a simple representation of this relationship.

FIGURE 8.2: A constructivist view of the relationships between teaching, learning and assessment

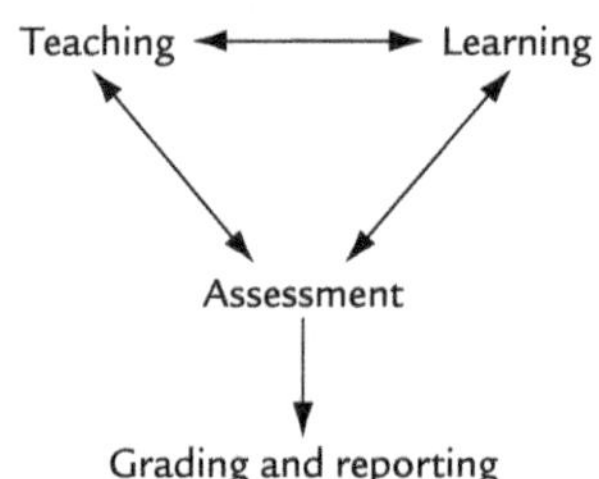

This constructivist model shows how teaching, learning and assessment have interactive relationships and there are roles for assessment to inform improvements in teaching and learning in addition to assessment of learning for grading and reporting purposes.

WHY DO WE ASSESS?

The purposes of assessment can be defined in terms of how the assessment information is used. The four main purposes for which assessment is conducted are:

- *Evaluative*. For evaluating curricula or for accountability purposes, such as benchmarking the performance of teachers, schools or systems against each other or against defined standards of performance.
- *Summative*. For determining the extent to which students have achieved learning outcomes and/or for certifying achievement and/or for selecting those students who will progress to the next level of education.
- *Formative*. For providing feedback to teachers and learners so that teaching and learning are improved.
- *Diagnostic*. To identify students' pre-instructional knowledge and alternative conceptions so that instruction can be planned to build on existing knowledge and to address students' alternative conceptions.

Of these four roles for assessment, classroom teachers are only directly involved in diagnostic, formative and summative assessment. However, it should be recognised that currently in Australia, the outcomes of national evaluative assessment programs such as NAPLAN and international student assessment programs such as TIMSS and PISA are a powerful influence on education policies and resourcing.

Diagnostic assessment

Diagnostic assessment is conducted at the beginning of a module or the beginning of a lesson. It is used to determine students' existing knowledge about the topic to be taught, and to identify students' alternative frameworks so that lessons can be planned to build on the pre-instructional knowledge of students and to challenge their alternative conceptions.

Good diagnostic assessment involves the use of probing, open questions that elicit students' understandings of the topic or concept of interest. In its simplest and most common form, teachers begin their lessons with a number of open questions to generate a whole-class discussion that reveals students' existing ideas and beliefs. Once the teacher has ascertained what students' existing ideas may be, the teacher leads the class into an exploration of the new concepts, taking an approach that fits with the students' existing level of knowledge.

A number of researchers have developed diagnostic assessment items that have been designed to elicit common alternative conceptions. Robin Millar and Vicky Hames (2003) have developed a set of items for a range of physical science topics that can be downloaded from the internet. Brenda Keogh and Stuart Naylor (2001) have developed a series of concept cartoons that use a cartoon to set a context and pose a question about a natural phenomenon, with three or four children giving their explanation about what is happening in the cartoon. Some of the views expressed provide alternative conceptions, while others offer a scientific explanation. The cartoons are used to stimulate discussion between students by asking them 'What do *you* think?' The Science Education Assessment Resources (SEAR) online database of assessment resources is also an excellent source of well-researched diagnostic items (see <http://cms.curriculum.edu.au/sear>).

One simple way of writing diagnostic items is to add an open question as a follow-up to a multiple-choice item that asks students to explain the reason for their choice of answer. The example presented in Snapshot 8.1 is based on the research conducted by Osborne and Cosgrove (1983) into students' ideas about the change of state of matter. The explanation provided to the follow-up question reveals students' beliefs about the composition of the bubbles.

Diagnostic items can be used on the interactive whiteboard to stimulate a whole-class discussion or printed out and used to stimulate small-group discussions. Disclosure of conceptions in these discussions makes both teacher and students aware of the range of conceptions existing in the class, and this can lead to investigations to test the various views held by the students.

SNAPSHOT 8.1: An example of a diagnostic assessment item

When water boils, large bubbles are formed.

Q1. What do you think is in the bubbles?

(a) air
(b) steam
(c) heat
(d) oxygen or hydrogen

Q2. Explain the reason for your answer.

Formative assessment

Formative assessment is used to provide feedback to teachers and learners so that teaching and learning are improved. Dylan Wiliam and others (eg. Black & Wiliam, 1998) have argued that five conditions must be met for assessment to be truly formative:

- A mechanism must exist for determining students' current level of achievement.
- A desired level of achievement, above the current level, is identified.
- The two levels are compared so that a gap is identified.
- The teacher provides prompts, scaffolding or support to inform students about *how* to close the gap.
- The learner uses the information to close the gap.

Formative assessment can be structured around the standards of achievement that are described in year levels as part of the *Australian Curriculum: Science* (ACARA, 2012). An example of the progression in learning of inquiry skills associated with evaluating investigations and formative feedback that can be provided by teachers is set out in Snapshot 8.2.

For students to be in control of their learning and produce quality academic work, they must have an understanding of the standard being aimed for, compare their current level of performance with the standard, and engage in appropriate action which leads to closure of the gap. Teachers therefore need to make information about standards

SNAPSHOT 8.2: Examples of formative feedback

Students need to reflect on their methods of investigation and identify possible ways of improving the design and conduct of the investigation as a way of enhancing their inquiry skills. In this example, students have been investigating factors influencing the bounce height of a tennis ball. The table shows the standards of achievement for evaluating investigations expected of Year 7–9 students. Examples of student responses to evaluation questions and how teachers might give formative feedback in the form of follow-up questions are illustrated below.

Year	Standards of achievement for evaluating investigations (based on ACARA, 2012)	Examples of students' responses	Examples of teacher's formative feedback
7	Students suggest improvements to their methods.	Make more accurate measurements.	How would you measure more accurately?
8	Students describe how improvements to methods could improve the quality of their results.	Make measurements at eye level to avoid parallax error.	You have used an appropriate measurement technique, but have inconsistent results. Why do you think your results are inconsistent?
9	Students identify inconsistencies in results and suggest reasons for uncertainty in data.	Sometimes the ball bounced on an uneven part of the brick paving.	Do you think you should discard the results for the bad bounces or should you do more repeat trials?

The teacher's responses take account of where the students are located on the learning continuum and what the next step is on the continuum, and then uses a question to scaffold students' thinking towards the next step along the learning journey.

explicit to students. Standards of performance can be communicated to students through descriptive statements, rubrics and/or exemplars.

One of the most effective ways of helping students understand the outcomes towards which they are working is to involve them in self- and peer-assessment. Students working in pairs using a rubric and commenting on each other's work can help them objectively compare their work to the standards described in the rubric and develop an understanding of the expected standards and what aspects of their work needs to be improved.

Research has shown that formative assessment is one of the most effective strategies for improving learning (Black & Wiliam, 1998); however, the key to its effectiveness is the quality of feedback given by teachers to students about their learning. Research by Butler (1988) demonstrates that feedback must be task-involving rather than ego-involving—that is, it directs attention to the task rather than to the self or ego. Butler showed that students given only comments improved their achievement significantly and all students had high interest in the work. Students given only grades showed no improvement in achievement, and those students who obtained high grades had high interest; however, those receiving low grades had low interest in the work. Giving grades and comments had no effect on achievement as students attended to the grades to the exclusion of the comments, and interest correlated with the grades received. The addition of praise with grades increased ego-involvement. To maximise achievement gains, feedback should therefore be limited to comments that describe what the student is doing well and what needs to be improved, and should give some guidance on how to improve the work.

Summative assessment

Summative assessment is used towards the end of a module, term, semester or year to determine the extent to which students have achieved the learning outcomes. Teachers use the information for grading or determining the level of achievement, and reporting to parents. Teachers typically use a range of evidence on which they will determine the students' grades for the semester. Sources of evidence usually include pencil-and-paper tests, quizzes or examinations, assignments, projects, reports of investigations and experiments, oral reports, work samples assembled into a portfolio and teacher observations of students' performance.

Cumulative approaches to collecting this evidence over a semester reduce the reliance on high-stakes end-of-semester tests, which create considerable stress and anxiety for students. Such tests only assess a sample of the important learning outcomes and advantage those students who can perform best under test conditions. Using a range of varied sources of evidence provides a more valid, reliable and equitable assessment of students' achievement in science.

WHAT SHOULD BE ASSESSED?

Assessment should focus on the learning outcomes that are of the greatest value to students so that teaching and learning address these outcomes. In the compulsory years of secondary schooling, there is universal agreement that science should focus on the development of scientific literacy. Scientifically literate citizens question, investigate, gather and analyse information, and make evidence-based decisions about themselves and their world (Goodrum, Hackling and Rennie, 2001). Being scientifically literate is more about being able to apply skills and understandings in everyday contexts to solve problems than simply acquiring a body of knowledge. Teaching, learning and assessment should therefore focus on those learning outcomes that contribute to scientific literacy.

It is also helpful to consider learning outcomes in terms of cognitive, psychomotor and affective domains. The cognitive domain includes knowledge and conceptual understandings, and intellectual skills such as the inquiry skills of science. These cognitive outcomes can be assessed at different levels—for example, simple recall, comprehension, application to new contexts, synthesis or evaluation. Most science assessments address cognitive learning outcomes. The psychomotor domain includes science manipulative skills and apparatus skills—for example, the skills involved in making accurate measurements. Psychomotor skills need to be assessed in a situation where the student performs the skill and the assessment is made by observing the performance or by checking the accuracy of results, such as measurements made. The affective domain includes attitudes towards science, such as like-dislike, trust-distrust, and scientific attitudes—for instance, objectivity in evaluating evidence. It is useful to survey students' attitudes towards science to gain feedback on their views so

that instruction and classroom climate can be modified to increase students' enjoyment and engagement with science.

HOW SHOULD WE ASSESS?

It is important to recognise that not all assessments need to be highly formalised. Diagnostic and formative assessments used for improving learning are usually informal and often spontaneous, occurring as the teacher interacts with students, observing their work and asking questions. These assessments require the teacher to have a rich knowledge of student learning and the developmental continuum leading to key learning outcomes so that the teacher can recognise where the student is on their learning journey and respond with appropriate prompts or questions that will help the student move forward. When highly reliable assessments are required for high-stakes decisions such as university admission, more formalised test-based assessment procedures are required to ensure reliability and to authenticate that the work has been produced by the student, rather than some other person.

There are a variety of ways of collecting evidence about students' learning. These include observation, closed-objective questions, open questions, exercises, projects and investigations, library and web-based research assignments and portfolios.

Observation and conferencing

Observation and conferencing are powerful and commonly used assessment procedures in primary school situations where the teacher works with the same class of students for extended periods of time. In secondary schools, observations and informal conversations with individuals are useful for collecting evidence from students with limited literacy skills who have difficulty in providing evidence in written form. Observations are also useful to note students who are able to perform certain skills during investigations—for example, controlling variables. These observations can be recorded directly by the teacher on the student's written work so that they are available when the student's work is collected for assessment. Evidence is most efficiently collected from secondary students through written work. Analysis of evidence collected in this way will reveal gaps that can be filled by observation and conferencing.

Closed-objective questions

Teachers will often include closed-objective questions such as true–false, fill-the-gap (cloze) activities and multiple-choice items on quizzes and tests, as they are quick and easy to mark. These types of item are useful for assessing students' mastery of basic content and facts, however, they are relatively ineffective in assessing higher order cognitive outcomes.

Open questions

To assess whether a student really understands science concepts, it is important to use open questions that require students to explain using their own words, and to set the question in a different context from that in which the concept was taught. This ensures that the student is required to apply the learning from the old context to explain in a new context using their own words rather than simply recalling the words used by the teacher without any real understanding. It must be recognised that the new context should be relatively similar to the old context and be familiar to the students, or the difficulty of the assessment will be increased considerably.

Exercises

Exercises such as analysing and interpreting secondhand data or conducting routine laboratory exercises and writing a report can be useful for gathering evidence about students' use of science process skills, such as constructing data tables and graphing.

Projects and investigations

Projects and investigations in which students plan and conduct their own investigations, and collect and analyse their data, are valuable approaches to collecting evidence about higher order inquiry skills that require the student to bring together conceptual understandings, science process skills and data in interpreting data and drawing conclusions, and in planning or critiquing the design of investigations.

Library and web-based research assignments

Not all research requires the collection of new data. Scientifically literate citizens should also be able to search for and select relevant existing

information about a question, and synthesise that information into a coherent report that can be communicated to others. Library and web-based research assignments are valuable tools for collecting evidence about these abilities.

Portfolios

Portfolios can be used to assemble a range of work samples to illustrate the growth in skills and understandings, and provide evidence of the current level of achievement. The major benefit of portfolios is that students can be actively involved in selecting work samples for inclusion that will illustrate their achievements. This raises their ownership of the work, increases their understanding of the learning outcomes to be achieved and enhances their awareness of their learning progress.

Once evidence has been collected, teachers must interpret and make judgements about the evidence. Marking schemes and rubrics are required to guide those judgements to enhance their accuracy and consistency.

Marking schemes

Marking schemes are usually devised by teachers for marking students' work, generating scores that are then used to award grades. Marking schemes tend to be of two types: global and analytical. Global marking is normally used in relation to judging the quality of performance outcomes (for example, an oral presentation) where a small number of broad criteria are used to guide the professional judgement made by the teacher. Teachers normally use a detailed marking key in analytical marking and assign marks to aspects of a work sample which are summed to give an overall mark for the piece of work. Detailed marking keys are particularly important to ensure consistency of marking of open-ended tasks and items. A sample task and marking key are shown in Snapshot 8.3 to illustrate one style of marking key.

Rubrics

Rubrics are devised by teachers, sometimes with students' involvement, and are used by students and by teachers working in standards-based

SNAPSHOT 8.3: An example of an open-ended assessment task and marking key

Assessment task

Write a short newspaper story (about two-thirds of a page) about the day when the world runs out of fossil fuels (about 175 years in the future). In your story, explain the history of energy use by humans and how future generations will meet their energy needs. Make sure you include a headline for your story.

Assessment marking key

Any valid points up to a maximum of 10 marks:

- Suitable headline (1 mark).
- Clarity and accuracy of communication in standard English (up to 2 marks).
- Wood an important early fuel for fires used for cooking and keeping warm (1), later supplemented by other fossil fuels such as coal (1).
- Industrial Revolution saw huge increase in use of fossil fuels such as coal and gas (1).
- The development of motor cars and petroleum-based fuels led to a huge increase in oil consumption (1).
- With concerns about the global warming (1) and increasing costs of fossil fuels, greater use made of nuclear energy (1) and renewable energy sources such as solar, wind and hydro (1).
- Great efforts made to increase the efficiency of energy use as costs of energy rise (1).

assessment schemes. Rubrics help students understand the learning outcomes they are striving to achieve, and the standards or steps along that learning journey. Students can use rubrics for self-assessment exercises. They help teachers to be clear about standards or levels of achievement and can provide a framework to guide both formative and summative assessment. Snapshot 8.4 illustrates a rubric used to guide the assessment of data-handling skills, including measurement, data recording and graphing.

SNAPSHOT 8.4: An example of an assessment rubric for data-handling skills

Data-handling skills	Grade		
	C	B	A
Measurement	Uses measurement when required and uses standard units of measurement, e.g. cm, kg.	Makes repeated measurements or uses replicates.	Trials the measurement procedure to improve its accuracy and uses apparatus that enhance accuracy, e.g. uses appropriate size measuring cylinder.
Recording data	Data are recorded using an appropriate form, e.g. lists, tables or diagrams.	Data recording is comprehensive, e.g. all trials are recorded.	Data recording uses an appropriate form, is comprehensive and uses appropriate conventions, e.g. tables have titles, column headings and units, independent variable recorded in left column and dependent variable in right column.
Graphing	Constructs bar graphs.	Plots bar and line graphs appropriate to the data type, i.e. line graphs when data for both variables are continuous.	When plotting line graphs, plots averages for repeated measurements, places the dependent variable on the vertical axis and uses appropriate scales with regular intervals.

HOW ARE GRADES ASSIGNED TO STUDENTS BASED ON MARKS?

Assignment of grades was traditionally norm-based–that is, a fixed percentage of students would be allocated different grades. For example, 10 per cent of students were awarded As, 25 per cent Bs, 30 per cent Cs, 25 per cent Ds and 10 per cent Es. Currently in Australia, grading is linked to standards of performance using grade-related descriptors. For example, to obtain an A grade in a Western Australian Stage 3 Year 12 course in Biological Science, the student must demonstrate the following standard of work in investigative and communication skills:

> Analyses a problem to formulate a hypothesis to be tested. Plans and performs scientific investigations with skill and initiative. Selects and uses appropriate resources and equipment efficiently and in a safe and correct manner. Collects data, assesses its validity and accuracy, organises it logically and presents it to reveal patterns and relationships. Explains abstract concepts and principles clearly using appropriate scientific terminology. (Curriculum Council of Western Australia, 2010.)

A common approach to marking and grading is to use analytical marking to award marks to pieces of work and then aggregate the student's scores across all assignments, tests and exams. Students are then rank ordered from those with the highest aggregate score to those with the lowest. Grade-related descriptors are then used to determine cut-off points between As and Bs, Bs and Cs, Cs and Ds, and Ds and Es. Work samples are often made available to illustrate different standards of work. Currently the *Australian Curriculum: Science* provides an achievement standard for each year level of the course and some exemplar work samples. At this stage, there are no resources equivalent to grade-related descriptors to help teachers make decisions about allocating grades.

WHAT ARE THE CHARACTERISTICS OF QUALITY ASSESSMENT?

Quality assessments should be valid, reliable, authentic, fair, comparable and educative. Each of these characteristics is considered in the following paragraphs.

Valid

Validity asks whether the assessment actually assesses what you intend to assess.

There are a number of aspects or types of validity. For teacher assessments, the two most important are content validity and construct validity. Content validity refers to the extent to which the assessments match the content and learning outcomes of the unit of work. This can be assured by preparing an assessment specifications grid in which you list the outcomes and content on one side of the grid, and the assessment tasks and items on the other side. By putting ticks in the boxes you can check the extent to which the assessment tasks match the outcomes. Construct validity refers to the extent to which the assessments really require students to use the understandings or skills intended to be assessed. Construct validity is checked by working through the tasks to determine the steps and reasoning required to complete each task. One of the most common threats to construct validity is the reading difficulty of the tasks. If reading difficulty prevents some students from understanding what they need to do, the task is placing more weight on the assessment of reading comprehension than the science.

Reliable

If students were given the same assessment task on two different occasions separated by a few days, and the results on the two occasions were the same, this would indicate that the assessment was highly reliable. Reliable assessments would produce the same student rankings on repeated administrations. Without reliability, a teacher cannot have any confidence in the results of assessments. With high-stakes assessments such as university entrance examinations, the assessments need to be highly reliable. The reality is that assessments of learning tend to be somewhat unreliable due to transient influences such as students' motivation, fatigue, guessing and practice effects. Guessing can be reduced by making all task and item instructions unambiguous and written with a reading comprehension level below that possessed by the students. There is a degree of error or uncertainty associated with all assessments. Such errors can be reduced by using a number of smaller assessments rather than a single high-stakes assessment.

Authentic

Some school assessments are decontextualised and involve contrived tasks that bear no relationship to the ways in which students will be expected to use the understandings and skills in their adult lives; such tasks lack authenticity. Authentic assessments are meaningful, contextualised in real-life situations, and require the application of skills and understandings that have long-lasting value in the person's life. Authentic assessments are often naturally integrated into the teaching-learning process. Authentic tasks assess things of value and, because they are meaningful to students, they are motivated to engage with them. Authenticity may require students to work in teams on certain tasks, which will require clearly established ways of sharing credit for the work between the participants.

Fair and equitable

The research literature (Parker & Rennie, 1998) indicates that student performance on assessments is strongly influenced by the test-taking situation, the response format of assessment tasks and the context within which the assessment tasks are set. These influences are also differential influences in that they may favour one sex over another. Formal, timed, competitive external examinations tend to favour males, whereas cumulative school-based assessments tend to favour females. Differences in test anxiety, social and communication skills are factors that have been used to explain these differences in performance. Multiple-choice items tend to favour boys, while extended-response items tend to favour girls. The extent of contextualisation of test items and the nature of the context can also selectively advantage some students over others. The greater the contextualisation of the task or question, the greater the demand for reading and graphical comprehension skills required to understand the question. Familiarity of context influences item difficulty; therefore, if the context is more familiar to one sex, socio-economic, geographical or ethnic group they will be advantaged over other groups (see Chapter 12 for more about equity in the science classroom). Assessment practices must allow all learners the opportunity to demonstrate what they know, understand and can do. Diversity in assessment practice allows all students the opportunity to demonstrate their learning accomplishments.

Comparable

Assessments made by different teachers and across different schools should be comparable in standards. The same work completed in different classes and assessed by different teachers should be assessed against the same outcomes and standards, and receive similar grades or levels of achievement. Comparability is enhanced when teams of teachers collaboratively prepare assessment tasks and marking schemes, some common assessment tasks are completed by all students, and teams of teachers mark samples of students' work and compare and modify their assessments until they reach a consistent standard in applying the marking scheme.

Educative

All assessments should in themselves be a learning experience so that students practice the application of valuable knowledge and skills in completing the tasks and receive feedback that guides future learning.

SUMMARY OF KEY POINTS

Assessment has a powerful influence over what is taught and learned, provides evidence for making decisions about students' educational futures and consumes a large proportion of teachers' time. Teachers should, therefore, think very carefully about why they assess, what they assess, how they assess and the quality of their assessments. As the primary purpose of schooling is to improve learning, assessment must focus strongly on providing feedback to teachers and students that is used for improving teaching and learning. To do this, assessment must be embedded within the teaching-learning process, rather than be tacked on the end of the learning sequence merely to measure the extent of learning. The fundamental purpose of science education in the compulsory years of schooling is to develop scientifically literate citizens. Science assessments should therefore focus on those learning outcomes that contribute to scientific literacy.

DISCUSSION QUESTIONS

8.1 What strategies would you use for diagnostic and formative assessment in a particular unit of work? Explain why you would use these particular strategies.

8.2 What steps could you take to ensure that your assessments are comparable with those of your colleages at your school, and with teachers at other schools?

8.3 Design a grid that you could use to plan the suite of summative assessment tasks you would use for a unit of work based on the *Australian Curriculum: Science*. What parameters would you use to frame the grid?

REFERENCES

Australian Curriculum, Assessment and Reporting Authority (ACARA) (2012). *The Australian Curriculum: Science*. Retrieved 24 November 2011 from http://www.australiancurriculum.edu.au/Science/Rationale.

Black, P., & Wiliam, D. (1998). Inside the black box: Raising standards through classroom assessment. *Phi Delta Kappan, 80*(2), 139–148.

Butler, R. (1988). Enhancing and undermining intrinsic motivation: The effects of task-involving and ego-involving evaluation on interest and performance. *British Journal of Educational Psychology, 58,* 1–14.

Curriculum Council of Western Australia (2010). *Guide to grades.* Retrieved 24 July 2011 from http://www.curriculum.wa.edu.au/Internet_Support_Materials/Guide_to_Grades.

Goodrum, D., Hackling, M., & Rennie, L. (2001). *The status and quality of teaching and learning of science in Australian schools.* Canberra: Department of Education, Training and Youth Affairs.

Hackling, M. W., Goodrum, D., & Rennie, L. (2001). The state of science in Australian secondary schools. *Australian Science Teachers Journal, 47*(4), 6–17.

Hattie, J. A. C. (2009). *Visible learning: A synthesis of over 800 meta-analyses relating to achievement.* London: Routledge.

Keogh, B., & Naylor, S. (2001). *Concept cartoons in science education.* Brisbane: Science Teachers Association of Queensland.

Millar, R., & Hames, V. (2003). *Diagnostic questions and how you might use them.* Retrieved 8 February 2004 from http://www.york.ac.uk/education/research/cirse/older/epse/resources.

Osborne, R., & Cosgrove, M. (1983). Children's conceptions of the changes of state of water. *Journal of Research in Science Teaching, 20*(9), 825–838.

Parker, L. H., & Rennie, L. J. (1998). Equitable assessment strategies. In B. Fraser & K. G. Tobin (Eds.), *International handbook of science education* (pp. 897–910). Dordrecht: Kluwer.

PART III
EXTENDING THE ART OF TEACHING SCIENCE

CHAPTER NINE

STUDENT ENGAGEMENT IN SCIENCE LESSONS

David Palmer

OUTCOMES

By the end of this chapter you will be able to:

- Explain why it is necessary to engage students in science
- Describe the factors that affect student engagement
- Describe the strategies of using novelty, personal relevance and success, and explain how to apply them in science lessons.

INTRODUCTION

Unfortunately, there is a declining interest in science among our youth. This may be surprising to those of you who are training to become secondary science teachers, as in the main you probably enjoyed science at school. However, the research suggests that many of your fellow high school students probably did not—it has been found that many secondary students perceive science to be a difficult and boring subject that has little relevance to their lives (Rennie, Goodrum &

Hackling, 2001). This situation can be expected to negatively impact upon students' scientific literacy, which not only requires a good understanding of science and scientific ways of thinking, but also the willingness and confidence to interact with science-related issues after they leave school. Researchers have also noted that enrolments in some post-compulsory science courses have steadily fallen (e.g. Lyons, 2006) and there is great concern about the low interest in science as a career, particularly among girls. However, research has also shown that negative attitudes can be changed to positive ones by teachers who consistently utilise strategies that foster engagement (Palmer, 2001). When you become a teacher, one of your challenges will be to aim for *all* your students to be positively engaged during your lessons.

It is easy to tell when students are highly engaged—they pay attention to the teacher, they begin working on tasks immediately, they follow directions, ask questions and volunteer answers, and they appear to be happy and enthusiastic. It must be emphasised, though, that engagement and learning are two separate things. Engagement does not guarantee that a student will learn what the teacher intended; it just means that the student is trying to learn. Teachers therefore need to not only use strategies that will result in engagement, but also strategies that will help students move towards more scientific understandings. The purpose of this chapter is to focus on the former—strategies that will result in engagement. The chapter will describe three main strategies that are supported by research—novelty, personal relevance and success—and will give examples of how they can be applied in science classrooms.

RESEARCH ON FACTORS AFFECTING ENGAGEMENT

There is no single theory of educational motivation that adequately describes all its features. Instead, different theorists focus on different factors that can influence motivation and engagement. For example, Ryan and Deci (2000) look at the differences between intrinsic motivation (that is, undertaking activities for their own sake) and extrinsic motivation (that is, undertaking activities in order to obtain a reward). Other theorists focus on the effects of interests and beliefs. For example, students who are interested in science—high individual interest—will be more likely to focus on opportunities to learn about science. Students who are confident they can learn science—high

self-efficacy—will be more likely to persevere when they are learning science. Students who want to understand the concepts—a mastery goal—or who want to demonstrate their proficiency in science—a performance goal—will be more likely to do what is required to understand or achieve in science. Students who expect that they will succeed and who value the learning of science—expectancy-value beliefs—will be more likely to try to learn science. Finally, students who believe that strenuous effort will result in success—a positive attribute—will be more likely to produce that effort.

Unfortunately, many adolescent students do not have a high interest in science or positive beliefs in relation to science. However, by using the three strategies of novelty, personal relevance and success, the aim will be to not only engage students in lessons but also to help build more positive patterns of interests and beliefs. The links between these three strategies and research are described in the following paragraphs.

Novelty

Novelty can occur when students experience something that is new, unusual or unexpected. *Intrinsic motivation* theorists argue that humans have innate psychological needs, including a need for novelty. This is strongly supported by *brain studies*, which have found that novelty directly results in production of the neurotransmitter dopamine, which has the immediate effect of focusing one's attention on the source of novelty (Niv, 2007). Thus novelty is a very powerful tool for gaining students' attention, which is an essential first step if engagement is to occur.

Personal relevance

This is the extent to which the content relates to the personal lives and adolescent interests of the students. The importance of personal relevance is supported by research on *individual interest*, as students choose to engage in activities that are of interest to them. It is also supported by *expectancy-value theory*, because students are more likely to become engaged when the content has personal value to them. Research has shown that personal relevance has a powerful effect on student engagement (Thompson & Windschitl, 2002), and it is considered to be an essential element of constructivist learning environments.

Success

According to *self-efficacy theory* (Bandura, 1997), when individuals experience regular successes in a task (such as learning science) they develop a strong self-confidence in their ability, and students with high self-confidence are more likely to persist until they succeed in understanding. The importance of success is also supported by *attribution theory*, because when students realise they can succeed if they apply effort, then they will be more likely to apply effort in the future.

Evidence from interviews with science students has also pointed to the importance of novelty, personal relevance and success. When students have negative attitudes towards science, it is usually because they consider it to be boring (lacking in *novelty*), difficult (lacking in experiences of *success*) and irrelevant (lacking in *personal relevance* to adolescents). The following sections describe how these ideas can be implemented in the classroom.

NOVELTY AND VARIETY

Novelty occurs when students encounter things that are new, unknown, unusual or unexpected. Variety is also a part of novelty, because it involves newness or change. Novelty can come from a range of sources in the classroom:

- *Information.* Surprising or unexpected information (for example, 'amazing' science facts) has high levels of novelty, whereas ordinary new information about the topic has moderate levels of novelty, and information that is already known to the students has low levels of novelty.
- *Hands-on activities.* Discrepant events demonstrations (that is, those that have a surprising result) are high in novelty, whereas experiments in which the results are highly predictable have moderate levels of novelty, and experiments in which the results are already known have low levels of novelty.
- *Pedagogical techniques.* A wide range of pedagogical techniques are available to teachers, including dramatisations, discussions, debates, model-making, problem-solving and open inquiry. Any technique that students have not experienced before will be high in novelty. When students experience appropriate variety in

pedagogical techniques within a lesson, and from lesson to lesson through the week, there will be acceptable levels of novelty, but when teachers consistently rely on teacher talk, writing notes or textbook reading at the expense of other techniques, there will be low levels of novelty.

- *Teacher behaviours.* A teacher who varies tone of voice, uses expressive gestures and varies location in the room is higher in novelty than a teacher who speaks in a monotone, has a passive body language and stands only at the front of the class.

Teachers should therefore make use of techniques such as 'amazing facts' and discrepant events activities, as well as using a variety of pedagogies and displaying active enthusiasm. A list of classroom examples of novelty is provided in Snapshot 9.1.

SNAPSHOT 9.1: Ways in which a teacher can introduce topic relevant novelty into science lessons

- Wear an unusual hat that relates to the topic (*creates the unusual*).
- Stop talking in the middle of a sentence (*creates the unexpected*).
- Bring an unusual artefact (such as a seahorse) to show the students (*creates the unusual*).
- Ask students to make private predictions about what they think will happen in a demonstration (*creates the unknown*).
- Ask a student to come to the front of the class to demonstrate something (*creates variety*).
- Put a relevant artefact in a box before the lesson, and tell students you will reveal it later in the lesson (*creates the unknown*).
- Explain a concept to the students then make a deliberate error in the notes that you give them—give an unexpected mini-treat to the first student who finds the mistake (*creates the unusual/unexpected*).
- Show students an amazing picture that relates to the topic (*creates the unexpected*).
- Ask a student to teach the class something (*creates the unusual*).
- Take students out of the classroom to learn something (*creates variety*).
- Tell students something that scientists *don't* know (*creates the unusual/unknown*).
- Change the seating in the classroom or change the posters/displays (*creates variety*).

- Tell students they *don't* need to know something (perhaps, today's most useless piece of information, but make it something interesting that relates to the topic) (*creates the unusual*).
- Have a physical activity break during the lesson (jump up and down, do a Tai Chi exercise, walk across the playing fields, do a hands-on activity) (*creates variety*).
- Dress as a stereotypical scientist and ask students to interview you about your latest discovery and to write it up as a newspaper article (*creates the unusual*).
- Teach the students a surprising science-based party trick that they can do at home (*creates the unexpected*).

Each of these teacher behaviours should relate closely to the topic. There is no point in telling the students an amazing fact that does not relate to the topic at hand, because it will just distract them. The main thing to remember about novelty is that you should try to make your classroom one in which the students are not quite sure what is going to happen next.

PERSONAL RELEVANCE

Although personal relevance has been shown to be a powerful motivator, surprisingly little is known about how best to enhance it in secondary science lessons. The following ideas are based on the small amount of research that has been done (e.g. Bonner, 2009) as well as further suggestions that can be trialled and modified by teachers.

A high level of personal relevance can be expected when the teacher relates the content to the personal lives and the general adolescent interests of the students. Conversely, low levels of personal relevance can be expected when the teacher relates science to real life issues that are not part of the students' lives or interests—for example, information about friction can be related to car engines, but if students have not looked at a car engine then it will have little impact on their engagement.

Of course, every student has their highly individual interests (one student may have a very strong interest in fashion design, whereas another may have a very strong interest in athletics), but if these interests are not shared by the other students in the class then it would be difficult for the teacher to use them when planning lessons. Instead, it would make more sense for teachers to utilise the issues that are of general interest to most adolescents, and these can be gleaned from adolescent popular culture. For example, stories about danger, romance and gender, celebrities, entertainment, music, food and wealth are likely to be of interest to most students (and indeed to most adults, as these topics make up much of the content of newspapers and television).

For most students, it therefore should be possible to create personal relevance by relating science content to these issues and topics, and also by linking science content to commonplace experiences that students have at home, or with family and friends. By doing some background research, the teacher can find ways to make these links. Snapshot 9.2 provides a list of ideas for making such connections.

SNAPSHOT 9.2: Ways of making science lessons relevant to students

Danger

- *Physics:* Smoke rises because of convection, so if you are in a house on fire, what should you do to avoid breathing smoke?
- *Chemistry:* Alfred Nobel was a chemist who studied explosives, and he was the inventor of dynamite. His younger brother was killed in an explosion at their factory.
- *Biology:* Many scientists have great courage. In 1900 Dr James Carroll suspected that mosquitoes carried the deadly disease yellow fever, so he bravely let an infected mosquito feed on him. He developed yellow fever, so the experiment was a success.

Romance/gender

- *Physics:* As a revision exercise, debate whether this physics topic was more relevant to women or to men.
- *Chemistry:* If you were a sodium ion, would you find yourself attracted to a chlorine ion? Why? Dramatise what happens when salt dissolves in water.
- *Biology:* During mating, the female praying mantis usually kills and eats the male. What would be the point of this?

Celebrities

- *Physics:* Comic actor Jack Black is the son of rocket scientists—his mother worked on the Hubble telescope.
- *Chemistry:* Brad Pitt belonged to the Forensics Club in High School.
- *Biology:* Nicole Kidman is reportedly scared of butterflies.

Entertainment

- *Physics:* Ask students whether they have ever seen an example of this physics concept in a movie.
- *Chemistry:* As a revision exercise, play a team version of a popular quiz show, using chemistry questions.
- *Biology:* Get students to think of a TV show that has an animal in it for at least one scene. Look at the credits to find out which company trained or provided the animals. Look them up on the internet. What sort of careers would this provide?

Music

- *Physics:* Use tuning forks to investigate sound vibrations.
- *Chemistry:* As a revision exercise, students choose their favourite song and replace the words with information about the current topic in chemistry. Perform it for the class.
- *Biology:* Some people have claimed that petunias (or grass seeds) grow better in response to different types of music. Students design an experiment to test this.

Wealth

- *Physics:* How could a person make money out of this physics topic?
- *Chemistry:* There are several kilograms of gold in each cubic kilometre of seawater. Design a way to collect it.
- *Biology:* Fossils are sold in shops in some tourist resorts—a mammoth tusk can cost up to $70 000, while a large fish or bird fossil can sell for $30 000. What would you have to do to make your living from fossils?

Food

- *Physics:* Teach students the test for rotten eggs (fresh eggs sink in water, but rotten eggs float due to gases released by bacteria).
- *Chemistry:* Use the internet to print out a recipe for your favourite meal. Identify all the places where a (change of state/chemical reaction/compound/mixture) occurs.
- *Biology:* Which parts of plants (roots, stems, leaves, flowers, fruit and seeds) did you eat for dinner last night?

The main thing to remember about personal relevance is that students are willing to pay money for it outside of school (by going to movies to see danger or romance) but you can provide it for free.

SUCCESS

Students experience a warm feeling when they know they have succeeded in something, and if this happens on a few occasions then they will be more likely to attempt future challenges in order to experience that rewarding feeling again. Thus frequent experiences of success will build strong engagement in the future. When teachers put in the groundwork early in the year, it pays off later in the year.

Success can come from a number of sources:

- *Success in understanding science.* This occurs when students feel they have learned something which they did not know before. It is arguably the most important form of success because it can occur in every science lesson.
- *Success in doing science.* This occurs when students perform a procedure effectively (such as being able to manipulate equipment in order to correctly carry out an experiment).
- *Success in assessment tasks and grades.* For some students, a passing mark will be taken as success, whereas others will look for a high grade, and others may simply wish to beat their peers.

In most cases, the success should be achieved only after students have applied some effort, as research has shown that automatic success (that which is not earned) is not effective. However, in your class you may have some students who have very low confidence and are not used to experiencing success—these students initially will need a series of very easy successes to start the process. In fact, a series of small successes is always much more effective than one or two big successes widely separated; students should therefore experience success of some sort on several occasions in each of your lessons. Below are some techniques for ensuring that students experience success.

- *Tell the students the goal for the lesson.* When students know where they have to get to in their learning, they will have a better chance of getting there. Then, when they do succeed, it will be apparent to them.

- *Provide simple, clear explanations.* Remember that many students are still coming to grips with scientific jargon, so carefully select the scientific terms you have to use, and leave out any that are not necessary. Pitch your explanation carefully to their level, so students don't feel it has gone 'over their head'. Look at their faces as you are explaining, and if you see confusion, stop and ask them about it. As many students need concrete experiences, the use of a variety of aids such as pictures, models, demonstrations and diagrams will usually assist them to experience success in understanding science.
- *Ask the students to express their comments, questions and ideas.* Success in understanding does not always result from simply listening to an explanation. In many cases, students need interaction with the teacher before they finally understand. Many secondary school students may be reluctant to ask a silly question or to say what they think in front of their peers, so you will need to encourage them. The first step is that you need to *stop talking*. Ask the students to talk to you. Wait. Ask them again. Wait some more. Then be very supportive when students do respond—for example, by smiling, using the students' names, nodding, listening attentively and thanking them. Sometimes you will need to correct them when they have expressed an idea that is not accurate, so do this by *praising their thoughtfulness*, then say, 'This is what a scientist would say . . .', as this is less of a failure than saying, 'You are wrong'.
- *Question the students about what they have just learned.* When the teacher shoots a few questions around the class, it is an opportunity to single out students for success when they answer correctly. It is important that teachers ensure this success by carefully designing questions that have an achievable level of difficulty for the individual students to whom they are asked. Sometimes students will not answer correctly, so you can give them prompts and reword the question until they get it right—don't move on to another student though, as this will deny success to the first student.
- *Ask students to demonstrate things to the class.* It can be challenging for students to come out the front and perform, so when they succeed they will feel good. Students can help you to perform a demonstration, or write something for the class, or argue a point. Sometimes a student will not succeed at first, so be prepared to prompt and hint until they do.
- *Give appropriate praise for effort, improvement and success.* Sometimes it can be difficult for students to judge when they have succeeded, so

you may need to tell them. Overt praise can occasionally be embarrassing to teenagers, who are very conscious of their peers, so use private praise if necessary—a quiet word, a gesture, a nod or an impressed look can be effective when overt praise is not working.

- *Ensure that hands-on activities work properly.* When experiments do not work properly, students often feel it is their fault, and it makes them feel like failures at doing science. Teachers should carefully check the available equipment before the lesson to make sure everything is working properly.
- *Circulate and provide assistance.* Students often need help as they do seatwork activities, so the teacher should circulate and provide enough assistance to ensure that *all* students succeed.
- *Assessment tasks should be flexible.* Assessment tasks can be modified so as to foster success:
  - Allow students to work at their own pace some of the time.
  - Allow failed students to resubmit or resit assessment tasks (and perhaps be given a maximum of a pass grade).
  - Provide additional assessment tasks, such as a quick quiz, that are specifically included to allow students to build success (although school policies may prevent these tasks from being a large part of their formal assessment).

The main thing to remember about success is that you should aim for every student to end the lesson feeling like a winner.

COMBINATIONS OF STRATEGIES

The effects of novelty, personal relevance and success can be very powerful when they are used together. The following are some examples of how this can be achieved.

- *Computer simulations.* Computer simulations are engaging for students, and this is arguably because they provide a strong source of novelty and success. Novelty can be provided by the creation of unusual situations such as frictionless worlds, in which real-world laws are not obeyed. Success can be provided by using a carefully graded series of scenarios, so students can experience a small success at each level, eventually experiencing success on many occasions. Each success provides a warm feeling of competence, which students would like to experience again, so it can become almost addictive.

- *Teacher personal anecdotes.* Personal anecdotes are stories from the teacher's real-life experiences that relate to the topic at hand. For example, as part of a unit on living things, a teacher might relate a story about going to Canada and seeing a bear. Students are usually very interested to listen to stories about a teacher's private life because they don't often have that opportunity, so it can provide novelty. It can also provide success because simple stories are easy to understand, and it can provide personal relevance because bears can be dangerous. Even if the anecdote does not contain danger, it is possible that students may find it personally relevant because it may provide an insight into how an adult lives their life, so adolescent students can relate it to how they would like to live their own lives.
- *Open inquiry.* Open inquiry occurs when students propose a question to investigate, design their methodology and carry out the experiment. It can create novelty, through the unusual nature of this technique; unfortunately, students are rarely allowed to do open inquiry. Similarly, much of the students' normal time at school is spent sitting, so any task that requires physical activity can be a good source of variety. Success in understanding science can occur because the hands-on component provides a concrete example that can illustrate the concept. Also, successful completion of a hands-on activity can allow students to experience success in doing science. Finally, open inquiry can provide personal relevance as students can choose ideas that interest them to investigate. This is actually how real scientists work. See Chapter 6 for more information about inquiry.

LIMITATIONS TO ENGAGEMENT

Engagement can be reduced when lessons are lacking in novelty, personal relevance and success, but there are several other factors that can also interfere with engagement. The first of these is students' *physical needs*, as in general students cannot become engaged in learning when they are hungry, over-tired, thirsty, uncomfortable or in pain. The second factor is *emotions*, as adolescents are prone to strong emotions, and when students come to class upset they will be less likely to be

able to focus on learning. Third, teenagers are particularly sensitive to the influence of *peers*—this influence can be positive when peers value learning, but it can be negative when classmates are resistant to learning. Finally, *distractions and interruptions* can also have a negative effect on engagement.

In summary, if there are occasions during which high-quality teaching is occurring but some students are not engaged, then factors such as physical needs, emotions and peers are likely to be responsible. Of course, it is not always possible to control student fatigue, hunger, emotions and so on, but the more these negative factors are minimised, the more the strategies of novelty, personal relevance and success will have a chance to be successful.

The ultimate form of teaching is to trick kids into learning something at the same time as they are enjoying themselves. Students do enjoy themselves if they are experiencing novelty, personal relevance and success. If they experience these things on a regular basis, then they will love coming to your classes and will be likely to develop into students who are interested in science and confident in their ability. You will really have opened their minds to the possibilities.

SUMMARY OF KEY POINTS

There is a need to enhance student engagement because many students find science lessons to be difficult, boring and irrelevant. Educational theory has suggested that engagement can be influenced by a wide variety of factors, including psychological needs, interests, self-efficacy beliefs, achievement goals, expectancies, values and attributions.

The strategies of novelty, personal relevance and success can be derived from these theoretical constructs. Novelty attracts students' attention. It can be provided by experiences containing the new, the unusual, the unexpected or the unknown, or by providing variety. Personal relevance has a powerful influence on engagement. It can be provided by relating science content to the lives of the students and to issues that are of general interest to adolescents. Success helps to make students want to learn more. It can be achieved when students understand scientific concepts, and when they perform experiments that work, as well as in assessment tasks.

Some teaching techniques, such as computer simulations, teacher personal anecdotes, and open inquiry are particularly engaging to students because they contain multiple sources of novelty, personal relevance and success. Engagement can be reduced if: students' physical needs have not been met, students are emotionally upset, there is peer pressure to disengage, or there are distractions and interruptions.

DISCUSSION QUESTIONS

9.1 Think of an engaging experience that you remember from high school science. Can you explain it in terms of novelty, personal relevance and success?

9.2 Think of an experience that was very demotivating for you. Can you explain it in terms of lack of novelty, personal relevance and success?

9.3 Look at the articles that would attract your attention in a newspaper. Do they contain elements of danger, romance and gender, celebrities, entertainment, music, food or wealth?

9.4 Talk to someone who didn't enjoy science at school, and try to understand the reasons. Can you explain it in terms of lack of novelty, personal relevance and success?

REFERENCES

Bandura, A. (1997). *Self-efficacy: The exercise of control.* New York: W. H. Freeman and Co.

Bonner, D. (2009). Establishing real-world connections for a better understanding of physics. *Physics Teacher, 47*(8), 490–492.

Lyons, T. (2006). The puzzle of falling enrolments in physics and chemistry courses: Putting some pieces together. *Research in Science Education, 36*(3), 285–311.

Niv, Y. (2007). Cost, benefit, tonic, phasic: What do response rates tell us about dopamine and motivation? *Annals of the New York Academy of Sciences, 1104*, 357–376.

Palmer, D. H. (2001). Factors contributing to attitude exchange amongst preservice elementary teachers. *Science Education, 86*, 1–17.

Rennie, L. J., Goodrum, D., & Hackling, M. (2001). Science teaching and learning in Australian schools: Results of a national study. *Research in Science Education, 31*, 455–498.

Ryan, R. M., & Deci, E. L. (2000). Intrinsic and extrinsic motivations: Classic definitions and new directions. *Contemporary Educational Psychology*, *25*, 54–67.

Thompson, J. J., & Windschitl, M. A. (2002, April). Engagement in science learning among academically at-risk girls: Sense of self and motivation to learn across learning contexts. Paper presented at the Annual Meeting of the American Educational Research Association, New Orleans, LA.

CHAPTER TEN

DEVELOPING A 'THINKING' SCIENCE CLASSROOM

Mary Oliver and Grady Venville

OUTCOMES

By the end of this chapter you will be able to:

- Critically analyse thinking skills programs
- Understand the theoretical basis of the Philosophy for Children and Cognitive Acceleration programs
- Apply strategies for developing a thinking science classroom

INTRODUCTION

There are seven general capabilities listed in the *Australian Curriculum* that are considered to be the skills, behaviours and attributes that students need to succeed in life in the twenty-first century. The capabilities include: literacy, numeracy, information and communication technology (ICT) competence, critical and creative thinking, ethical behaviour, personal and social competence, and intercultural understanding. These general capabilities are to be embedded across

all content areas of the curriculum, including science. The focus of this chapter is on critical and creative thinking. The conceptual statement for the *Australian Curriculum* critical and creative thinking general capability can be found at <http://consultation.australiancurriculum.edu.au/GeneralCapabilities>. This document explains that:

> In the Australian Curriculum students develop critical and creative thinking as they learn to generate and evaluate knowledge, ideas and possibilities, and employ these skills when seeking new pathways or solutions. In the context of schooling, critical and creative thinking are integral to activities that require reason, logic, imagination and innovation. In learning to think broadly and deeply students employ reason and imagination. (2011, p. 1)

The critical and creative thinking general capability incorporates four interrelated processes, including: (1) inquiring; (2) generating and developing ideas and possibilities; (3) analysing, evaluating and synthesising information; and (4) reflecting on thinking, actions and processes.

While thinking is now embedded in the *Australian Curriculum*, for teachers it is not always clear how such skills can be delivered and evaluated, or even how they impact students' learning. For all teachers in general, and for science teachers in particular, encouraging and supporting their students to be able to think critically and creatively should be an important and well-developed part of their classroom pedagogy. The purpose of this chapter is to consider how we might develop and support a 'thinking' science classroom. The chapter is presented in three sections. In the first section, we examine the evidence for 'brain-based' or 'thinking' educational programs, in particular considering evidence from the field of neuroscience. In the second section, we look in depth at two thinking programs that have been shown through research to promote learning and cognition in children, the Philosophy for Children (P4C) program and the suite of programs referred to as Cognitive Acceleration (CA) programs, or Cognitive Acceleration through Science Education (CASE). In the third section, we explore two approaches that can be used during lesson planning and in the classroom to support critical and creative thinking, including Bloom's Taxonomy and questioning techniques.

WHAT IS THE EVIDENCE FOR THINKING SKILLS PROGRAMS?

Teaching is an old and noble profession, embedded with a history of ideals of social equity, justice and optimism. 'Traditional' or anecdotal methods of teaching are often legacies inherited from previous generations of school teachers. As teachers of science, however, we are familiar with scholarly practice in science that has done much to advance the knowledge economies of the world. We should be confident about improving the quality of teaching and learning through applying the principles of science to teaching through developing evidence-based practice, using results from research to inform practice and maintaining commitment to professional learning with regard to best practice. For example, research has shown that teachers need to be aware of the possible alternative conceptions students bring to their classrooms, that learning is an 'inside the individual' process that builds on prior knowledge, and that it is something that can be facilitated through social interaction with peers and more knowledgeable people. Considerable evidence was presented in Chapters 2 and 3 about the value of this knowledge and how it can be used to build evidence-based practices for the teaching and learning of science. In a similar way, teachers need to be able to evaluate the range of 'brain-based' or 'thinking' programs that are promoted within educational settings. Neuroscience is a good place to start contemplating the evidence for and against these programs.

Neuroscience informing educational approaches

Clearly the human brain is the central organ of learning and development, and as a consequence teachers and educators are interested in the cognitive and other developments of the students they teach. Until recently, however, there has been little collaboration between neuroscientists and educational researchers, and information available to teachers about the ways the brain works and how that can inform teaching practices has been scant. Neuroscience 'investigates the processes by which the brain learns and remembers, from the molecular and cellular levels right through to brain systems' (Goswami, 2004, p. 1). With improved brain imaging techniques, there has been unparalleled growth in neuroscience research in recent years. As a consequence, neuroscience has contributed enormously to our understanding of attention, stress, memory, exercise and sleep. Research in the

field of educational neuroscience is being used to understand how the brain develops and functions, in the diagnosis of neurological conditions (which then allows for early remediation), and in the evaluation of intervention programs. Unfortunately, the practical application of 'brain-based' findings in education seems to be dominated by highly marketed, instead of evidence-based, programs (Stephenson, 2009). A number of myths have grown up around brains, some of which have permeated education.

The myths about brains that seem to be prevalent in educational circles include, but are not limited to, the following four examples.

1. *Critical periods of learning* (OECD, 2007).
   - The idea that there are critical periods of learning, or narrow periods during development to which learning certain skills or thinking abilities is restricted, may have its origins in studies of rats maintained in low-stimulus environments whose brains showed low synaptic density, or imprinting studies in young birds.
   - No critical periods of learning have yet been found in humans. There may be 'sensitive' rather than 'critical' periods for learning. For example, studies on very young children have shown that they are responsive to sounds produced by a variety of different language groups. This responsiveness is 'lost' unless the child hears the sounds regularly as part of his or her linguistic environment.
2. *Multiple intelligences (MI); 'Brain Gym®'* (Stephenson, 2009) *and learning styles* (Crossland, 2008).
   - Renowned educators such as Edward De Bono, Howard Gardiner and Lane Clarke have contributed to raising awareness of the need for 'critical thinkers' and of the role schools play in facilitating change and development in student thinking.
   - Based on the general discussions and theories promoted by these educators, teachers are often urged to encourage their students to use 'thinking hats' to solve problems, to spiral different 'thinking types' so they ensure that various multiple intelligences are addressed in students through the design of the curriculum, and to encourage students to participate in brain exercises or 'gym'.
   - There is no evidence to date to support the claim of a preferred learning style, and even when the supposed preferred learning

style is used, there is no evidence of educational improvement (Crossland, 2008).
- There is no evidence to support the idea that using multiple intelligences in the classroom improves learning or cognition (Crossland, 2008).
- There is no evidence to show that the program Brain Gym® makes any difference to students' brains, cognition or achievement (Stephenson, 2009).

3. *Only about 10 per cent of our brains are used at any time.*
   - This myth is often attributed to Einstein, but more likely emerged from the neurologists in the nineteenth century who found that only about 10 per cent of neurons are active at any one time.
   - Imaging studies have shown that brain activity is disparate and can be very 'precisely described' (OECD, 2007, p. 113).
4. *We are either right-brain or left-brain learners.*
   - Although the two hemispheres control different parts of the body and have discrete functions, both are employed and co-ordinate activities together.
   - When the two hemispheres are separated, there follows loss of brain function and capacity.

The prevalence of programs in schools that are not supported by evidence adds to the confusion for teachers, parents, students and administrators. Sylvan and Christodoulou (2010) provide an evaluative tool to assess the educational merit of commercially available brain-based learning products, cautioning that educational programs need to be evidence based, and that they should bring about measurable behavioural changes (which in usual terms might mean improved student behaviour, well-being or achievement) and have a sustained impact.

EVIDENCE-BASED PROGRAMS THAT PROMOTE THINKING

Recent analysis of the large body of published research in education shows that some thinking skills programs do improve the performance of students on cognitive and curriculum tests (Higgins, Baumfield & Hall, 2007). A number of meta-analyses point to a very limited number of programs that demonstrably improve students' thinking.

'Philosophy for Children' is one such program and the Cognitive Acceleration (CA) programs such as 'Thinking Science' and 'Let's Think!' are others. These programs are helpful to teachers and powerful in improving the quality of the learning experience for students. They demonstrate that teaching to promote thinking is demanding of both teachers and students. In the next two sections, we review each of these evidence-based programs, explore what lessons in these programs look like and consider how these lessons might benefit the students.

Philosophy for Children (P4C)

Developed by Matthew Lipman as a response to undergraduate students' difficulties in thinking and reasoning, Philosophy for Children aims to improve thinking and reasoning skills in school students (see <http://cehs.montclair.edu/academic/iapc/whatis.shtml>). Philosophy as a discipline is about the cultivation of excellent thinking, and involves the active exploration of puzzling and debatable ideas and concepts. Given that so many of the big issues that face the world today—such as global warming, over-population and genetic engineering—are debatable, with no clear answers, it is not surprising that philosophy is regaining importance in educational circles.

What P4C lessons look like

Curriculum materials in P4C have been published for children from Kindergarten to Year 12. Children participating in P4C are encouraged to think about thinking, about nature, about ethics and about reasoning. For example, one P4C module aimed at primary school children emphasises relationships, including logical, social, familial, aesthetic, causal, part-whole and mathematical relationships. In middle school (Years 5 to 8), another P4C module involves students in discussions about animal rights, sexism, racism, justice, divorce and death. In high school (Years 9 to 12), another module about reasoning in the language arts considers concepts like friendship, freedom, integrity, originality, harmony, form, balance, personhood and meaning. The P4C sessions have four important elements:

1. They begin with a stimulus. This is often a narrative with an intriguing element—essentially something to 'spark' off some philosophical thinking.

2. Students are given time to reflect on the stimulus. Then, working together in small groups, they start to formulate some philosophical questions.
3. The whole class considers questions, then selects one for the general philosophical discussion. The teacher guides or facilitates the discussion, ensuring that all students are engaged.
4. Finally, students participate in a reflection on both the ideas and the process of inquiry.

Creating such a thinking classroom for students to become intellectually more confident and competent requires considerable facilitation by the teacher. An important idea underpinning the P4C approach is the development of a 'community of inquiry'. When teachers model the sort of Socratic or philosophical questioning that is encouraged by P4C and engage with the inquiry, as well as guide students, inevitably there is greater focus on what students think and more student talk, leading to a more dialogic classroom—that is, a classroom with dialogue that goes back and forth, with more than one person actively contributing to the discussion. Participating in the community of practice and inquiry through P4C is a social process, which requires students to share their own perspectives, read faces, listen to one another, challenge and build on each other's thinking, consider missing perspectives and reconstruct their own ideas. The developers of P4C claim that most students find this kind of meaningful classroom interaction and discussion irresistible: they can't help joining in, contributing their own ideas and reflections. In this way, cognitive and social skilfulness are acquired in context, in a natural way, rather than through forced drills. See Snapshot 10.1 for an example of a program that does just that.

SNAPSHOT 10.1: Teaching philosophy in Sydney

Philip Cam at the School of History and Philosophy at the University of New South Wales has been actively promoting the teaching of philosophy in schools. See <http://www.youtube.com/watch?v=tk_B32HtnWg> for an interesting YouTube clip of Australian children from Stanmore Public School in Sydney participating in philosophy with insights from Philip Cam.

How do the P4C lessons benefit students?

Evidence from the 1970s has shown that even short courses using the P4C materials and inquiry-based pedagogical approach have resulted in improved logic and reasoning skills (Lipman, 1976). Teachers reported showing improved thinking skills such as inquiry, questioning and communication (Fisher, 2001). Philosophy offers a means of engaging students as a 'community of enquiry, in which children are exposed to and internalise the skills and habits of higher order thinking' (Fisher, 2001, p. 67). As well as addressing issues such as literacy in primary schools, philosophy enables teachers to plan deliberately for metacognitive activities, that is, activities where the student thinks about and reflects on their own thinking and learning in the classroom. As one student said, 'you should listen to other people because sometimes they have good ideas' (Fisher, 2001, p. 73) .

According to Lipman (2003), participating in a community of inquiry captivates young people in important cognitive activities such as creating hypotheses, asking for and giving good reasons, clarifying their terms, offering examples and counter-examples, drawing inferences, questioning each other's assumptions and pursuing a line of inquiry. By teaching with this sort of inquiry-based approach, Lipman (2003) claims a spectrum of different skills will be enhanced, including 'cognitive skills, making distinctions, seeing connections, identifying fallacies, finding analogies/disanalogies, seeing broader perspectives, formulating and testing criteria, sticking to the point, open mindedness, being willing to offer and accept criticism, valuing reasonableness, increasing tolerance against opposing ideas and drawing inferences' (2003, pp. 167–71).

P4C in Australia

Now firmly established in school education systems overseas, P4C is being developed across Australia through universities (see <http://www.uq.edu.au/hprc/index.html?page=21377>) or schools acting as centres (see <http://burandass.eq.edu.au/wcmss/index.php/Philosophy-Training.html>). Curriculum materials are available for K–12 and managed in Australia through the Federation of Australasian Philosophy in Schools Association (see <http://www.fapsa.org.au/about-us>) and ACER (see <https://shop.acer.edu.au/acer-shop/group/QAQ/38;jsessionid=46D7336122F020063948316DF64390D8>).

Cognitive Acceleration through Science Education (CASE), or Thinking Science

A suite of cognitive acceleration programs were developed in response to research that showed that focused teaching can influence children's general cognition or ability to think. The original program was called Cognitive Acceleration through Science Education (CASE) and has been commercially developed into a program called Thinking Science (Adey, Shayer & Yates, 2001). Thinking Science is a series of 30 'thinking' lessons that are delivered to Year 7, 8 or 9 children, usually by their science teachers, once a fortnight over two years. The theory underpinning the cognitive acceleration programs embraces both Piagetian and Vygotskian schools of thought. Piagetian theory details the stages of cognitive development through which children go as they mature and learn, and this is used to inform the level or degree of difficulty for the Thinking Science lessons. Vygotskian theory contributes the idea that specifically targeted problems which require problem-solving and thinking in a zone just beyond what the child is already capable of will result in cognitive conflict, and thus promote learning. Reasoning patterns specifically addressed through the activities of the Thinking Science materials include controlling variables, ratio and proportionality, compensation and equilibrium to analyse process, using correlation, probability, determining criteria for classification, using formal models of thinking and understanding compound variables. Thinking Science is structured in such a way that the lessons spiral through increasing levels of complexity of these reasoning patterns.

What a Thinking Science lesson looks like

Thinking science lessons usually take between 50 minutes and one hour of classroom time, and include five key components:

1. *Concrete preparation* involves the teacher establishing a problem for the students to consider and to negotiate any associated ideas and terminology needed to understand the problem.
2. *Cognitive conflict* is a process whereby students are encouraged to think about the problem in a way that challenges their conventional ways of thinking. Students are encouraged to consider a range of possible explanations for the problem.
3. *Social construction* is the shared development of explanations of and understandings about the problem and potential solutions.

Teachers play a role in establishing suitable small groups and asking probing questions of students but not offering solutions. Active participation by all students is required, as all are expected to negotiate explanations and solve problems.
4. *Metacognition* involves students reflecting on their thinking and articulating their approaches taken to problem-solving, thus enabling other students to access other ways of thinking and evaluating.
5. *Bridging* involves applying the ideas developed to other problems in the real world. Associated science lessons can be used to help reinforce and remind students about the range of problem-solving strategies and ways of thinking they develop during these lessons.

The Thinking Science activities are based on Piagetian reasoning patterns, as described above. For example, one of the first lessons in the reasoning pattern of controlling variables requires students to consider the variables and values within a set of different shapes of different sizes and colours. Teachers put the students into small groups to complete the activities, probe with questions, and encourage students to articulate their reasons and explanations within the small groups, then as a whole class. This sort of setting, where no one in the group knows the answer, but peer discussion enhances understanding for all participants, allows students to develop communicative and metacognitive skills (Smith et al., 2009). The construction of knowledge in a group setting through participation in and reflection on the issues related to the activity paves the way for the learning to be internalised by each individual student. The individual student's thinking and learning thus reflect the quality of collective thinking.

How do Thinking Science lessons benefit students?

The evidence of the effect of the CASE program on students' cognitive growth and academic achievement has been published in a number of forms over the years. The original CASE experiment, with only about 130 students, as well as more recent work, with over 2000 students from eleven schools (Shayer & Adey, 2002), both demonstrated that students participating in the CASE program during Years 7 and 8 showed improved cognition on Piagetian-based reasoning tasks compared with students in control schools. Moreover, the improvement was sustained and impacted on performance at the (UK) General Certificate of Secondary Education (GCSE) results three years after the program had ended, not only in science but also in mathematics and English. Thinking Science is currently being implemented in schools in Australia (see Snapshot 10.2 for more details).

SNAPSHOT 10.2: Thinking Science Australia

Teachers from across Australia are working with the Thinking Science activities in their classrooms, implementing the CASE program. A two-year professional learning program to support schools and teachers implementing these activities is now available in Australia through the University of Western Australia (<http://www.education.uwa.edu.au/tsa>). These lessons are very different from the usual science lessons, and teachers often preface the lessons with the requirement that students only have to do two things: 'think and participate'.

After a year of participating in Thinking Science lessons, one Year 8 student said: 'I felt smarter and pleased that I learned something.' This student also explained that the lessons were hard work—for example, 'thinking how we got our answers'. He further explained how the lessons impacted on his thinking and approach to science: 'Now when we do an investigation, I look at the questions with a different attitude/state of mind.' Participating Australian science teachers have already noted an improvement in students' performance in investigative tasks by the end of the first semester.

STRATEGIES TO SUPPORT HIGHER ORDER AND CRITICAL THINKING

In this section, we explore two broad and related strategies that are important for supporting and promoting higher order and critical thinking in the classroom. The first is the use of Bloom's Taxonomy, and the second is the use of questioning in the classroom.

Bloom's Taxonomy

As a teacher, you will often hear the phrase 'higher order thinking'. In order to explore what higher order thinking means and how this concept can be used to support thinking in the science classroom, we will explore Bloom's Taxonomy. Bloom (e.g. Bloom et al., 1950) and other educational theorists (e.g. Anderson & Krathwolh, 2001) developed a hierarchy of different types of knowledge. The hierarchy can be used in education to indicate simple and complex learning behaviours. The complex learning behaviours are said to require 'higher order thinking'. Knowing facts and comprehending information are considered the most simple forms of knowledge, while applying, analysing, evaluating and creating are higher levels of learning requiring higher order thinking. Table 10.1 provides an overview of this hierarchy with an explanation of each level and examples of learning behaviours associated with that level. Each level includes the lower levels but requires a more complex type of thinking.

TABLE 10.1: An overview of the revised Bloom's Taxonomy with higher levels of thinking in descending order

Level of thinking	Description	Types of instructive behaviour
Knowledge	Remembering and recalling previously learned information	List, write, define, name, state, describe, identify, select, label
Comprehension	Demonstrating an understanding of information by translation, interpretation or extrapolation	Convert, explain, illustrate, predict, summarise, defend, estimate
Application	The application of abstract or theoretical principles and ideas to different situations	Use, construct, apply, solve, modify, relate, prepare, show
Evaluation	The ability to make value judgements based on evidence and clearly defined and systematically applied criteria	Critically determine, judge, appraise, compare, conclude, discriminate, interpret, contrast, relate
Creation	Generating new ideas, products or ways of viewing things. It might involve identifying the parts and clarifying relationships between them	Design, construct, plan, invent, compare and contrast, deconstruct, identify causes, differentiate, infer

Bloom's Taxonomy is helpful for teachers to be able to analyse the kinds of thinking that different classroom activities prompt in their students. Classroom activities that require students to recall facts and knowledge may sometimes be important, but they only require lower order thinking. For example, it may be helpful for students to label the parts of a millipede, or to state the second law of thermodynamics, but these activities will not improve the students' thinking skills. It is also important for teachers to use activities in the classroom that require higher order levels of thinking. For example, students could infer the results of continued population growth (comprehension), distinguish fact from assertion in an experiment (analysis) or evaluate the evidence for human influence on global warming (evaluate). Bloom's Taxonomy is also useful for lesson planning and programming (see Chapter 5), to ensure that students are involved in a range of activities that require thinking at all levels at least some of the time. Teachers can also use Bloom's Taxonomy to reflect on and plan their classroom questioning techniques and strategies. In the next section, we look more closely at questioning and ways teachers can use questions to optimise thinking.

Asking better questions

Transmission styles of teaching involve much talk and questioning from the teacher. They also give the impression that the teacher possesses all the knowledge. Some teachers ask many 'knowledge'-type questions in their classrooms, as if they have an internal script with students supplying the occasional one-word answers. For example: What is the chemical symbol for nitrogen? To what phylum do crocodiles belong? What is the third planet from the Sun? We call these questions 'closed questions' because there is only one correct answer and they only require students to recall information and not engage in higher order thinking. Closed questions may be useful for revision for a test, for classroom management purposes or for leading students through a logical process; however, they are unlikely to either engage the entire class or drive learning. Of course, without knowledge, we are not able to use higher order thinking skills such as analysing, evaluating or synthesising, but it is also important for teachers to ask questions that will require higher order thinking. Compare the previous questions with the following higher order questions: How are chemical symbols useful to scientists? What are the differences and similarities between the vertebrate and invertebrate phyla?

Chin (2007) researched the range of questions constructivist teachers tend to use and found detailed examples of questions to promote greater student participation and response, and ultimately something she referred to as 'productive thinking'. Table 10.2 provides a summary of some of these types of question, their features, when they are used and examples. From Table 10.2, we can see that Socratic questioning can be used to prompt and guide students through a process (What step should we take next? Why?) or to encourage them to provide more information (Why do you think that? Can you give a reason to support your answer?). A framing approach to questions requires an over-arching question or problem and sub-questions that help students to see the links between a big issue, system or concept and more subordinate concepts or ideas (such as the relationship between respiration and cells and mitochondria). The examples in Table 10.2 indicate that improving thinking and engagement in students requires us to ask more searching questions. Is there any evidence that particular methods of asking questions are more effective in promoting learning?

Asking questions and 'wait time'

A large body of evidence has been amassed about teachers' questions, in particular how long the 'wait' interval is between the teacher's question and the student's response and before another question (Rowe, 1986). Teachers wait, on average, only 1.5 seconds for a response (2 seconds for high-ability and 0.9 seconds for low-ability students) and if there is no response, they often ask yet another question. If teachers allow more time (3–5 seconds) for students to think, more students contribute with more extended statements, forming discussions rather than one-word responses. If teachers allow more time, the quality of the questions also change, with teachers more likely to ask for student clarification, justifications or evidence, or to invite elaboration of contrary positions (Rowe, 1986). All these things lead to a cognitively richer classroom environment, involving more students in the dialogue of ideas and reduced teacher talk. Such a simple strategy of extending wait time has a profound impact on both teachers and students in creating a classroom where the exchange of ideas occurs.

TABLE 10.2: Questioning techniques used by constructivist teachers to promote productive thinking

Question type	Features	When used	Classroom example
Socratic questioning	• Use a series of questions to prompt and guide student thinking • Encourage students to provide more information	• To encourage students to generate ideas based on reasoning and prior knowledge • To foster student talk • To encourage student to reflect on answer	For an investigation on density, one teacher used a series of questions to prompt and guide the students' thinking rather than telling them a list of instructions. Some of the classroom dialogue is included below. *T:* How will the athlete know if his gold medal is made of pure gold? *S1:* Find the density of the gold. *T:* Find the density of the gold. How can we find that out? *S1:* Find the mass. *T:* We need to find the mass first. How do we find the mass? *S1:* We use the weighing machine, an electronic balance. *T:* By using an electronic balance ... what do we need to do next? *S2:* Find the volume. *T:* You need to find the volume and how do you find the volume? *S3:* Use a displacement can. *T:* So now we've got the mass and the volume. What do we do with these two values to work out the density? *S4:* Mass divided by volume. *T:* Mass divided by volume, okay, so we've got the density of the medal, what do we do next?

Verbal jigsaw	• Focus on the use of scientific terminology, keywords and phrases to form integrated propositional statements • Guide students to form a series of propositional statements to form a coherent mental framework	• For topics with several technical terms; for students with weak language skills • To introduce factual or descriptive information and to reinforce scientific vocabulary	In a lesson on mitosis, a teacher provided students with diagrams of each stage. Rather than just checking whether the students put the stages in the correct order, she asked questions to help them understand and use the new terminology and justify why they put the diagrams in a particular order. The following question were used: • Would anyone like to try to explain how you figured that out? • What's the difference between diagram B and diagram C? • What is each one of these? [chromatids] • What do these ball-and-stick figures represent? • What do you notice about these four chromosomes? • How are they being paired up?
Semantic tapestry	• Help student weave disparate ideas together into a conceptual framework, like constructing a tapestry of ideas • Guide students to think at both the macro-level and at the micro- or	• To focus on ideas and abstract concepts • To help students view a problem from different angles and perspectives • To help students to understand	When teaching about the density of ice in comparison with water, a teacher asked the following questions to help the students weave together the ideas of mass, volume and density, and link these macroscopic ideas with what is happening at the molecular level: • If ice floats on water, what does that tell you about the density of ice? • Why is ice less dense than water? • When it expands, what happens to the volume of ice? • What happens in an ice tray when water freezes—does it sink in or bulge out?

(cont.)

Question type	Features	When used	Classroom example
	molecular level, or use questions that zoom in and out	a concept at both the macro-, overarching level and the micro-, in-depth level	• Which quantity changes: the volume or the mass? • What happens to the density as the same mass of water changes into ice? • What happens to the molecular packing? Are the molecules still as close as before? • So what happens to the number of molecules it can pack into the same volume? • If you have fewer molecules in the same volume, what happens to the mass per unit volume? And the density?
Framing	• Use questions to frame a problem, issue or topic and to structure the discussion • Present a big, broad question and subordinate or related questions visually (e.g. on slides)	• To help students see the relationship between a big question, concept or problem and the information that it addresses • To visually focus students' thinking and help them see the links between the big question and the subordinate questions	In an introductory lesson on respiration, a teacher set the students a few problems or 'thinking tasks' that were set as an over-arching trigger question and a series of sub-questions. Students worked in small groups and then presented their answers to the class. *Over-arching problem:* • Imagine you are an oxygen particle. Trace the path taken by the oxygen particle, beginning from the nose to the cell. *Sub-questions:* • What happens to the oxygen particle in the alveolus? • What would be the final destination of the oxygen particle? • What happens in the cell? • What is the chemical process that occurs in the cell? • What is the purpose of this chemical reaction?

Source: Adapted from Chin (2007, pp. 823–36).

SUMMARY OF KEY POINTS

What seems to be common to both the Cognitive Acceleration and Philosophy for Children programs are the requirement for teachers to play a different role in the classroom—as more of a Socratic interlocutor than a transmitter of factual information. The key principles that seem to be most evident in these successful 'thinking' programs are:

- *Cognitive challenge:* A problem that is too difficult for each student to think about on their own.
- *Social construction of knowledge:* Focused collaboration with peers to solve the problem.
- *Metacognition:* Reflection on the problem-solving and the process.

During the activities examined in this chapter, students are required to work together to solve difficult problems and the teacher's role is to probe and to ask questions such as: 'How did you work that out?' or 'Tell us how you worked that one out' or 'What do we need to think about when we are doing this?' As a result, students are required to reason about the problem as well as their own thinking. These types of questions are not 'closed' in the sense that teachers do not seek right or wrong answers; rather, their role is to assist and push the thinking with the skilful and judicious use of questions.

While thinking activities themselves are essential components of programs that improve students' thinking and impact on their achievement, the real difference lies in the quality of the teaching that accompanies their use. Teachers need professional support and coaching to implement credible thinking programs and to be supported over a long period. There is a need for studies to bring scientific evidence to evaluate educational strategies as well as bridge the education neuroscience divide that currently exists. In this sense, the application of evidence-based practice could do for education what it has achieved in medicine.

DISCUSSION QUESTIONS

10.1 What strategies can you use in your lesson plans to demonstrate teaching for thinking?

10.2 How can you ensure you allow sufficient 'wait time' in your lessons?
10.3 Identify which thinking skills (e.g. inquiry, knowledge, reasoning, analysis, evaluation) you are currently targeting in your teaching and explain how you are doing this.
10.4 How could you evaluate whether a 'brain-based' program has scientific or educational merit?

REFERENCES

Adey, P., Shayer, M., & Yates, C. (2001). *Thinking science: student and teachers' materials for the CASE intervention* (3rd edn). London: Nelson Thornes.

Anderson, L. W., & Krathwohl, D. R. (Eds.) (2001). *A taxonomy for learning, teaching, and assessing: A revision of Bloom's Taxonomy of Educational Objectives.* New York: Longman.

Bloom, B. et al. (1950). *A Taxonomy of Educational Objectives: Handbook 1—The cognitive domain*. New York: David McKay.

Chin, C. (2007). Teacher questioning in science classrooms: Approaches that stimulate productive thinking. *Journal of Research in Science Teaching, 44*(6), 815–843.

Crossland, J. (2008). The myths surrounding 'brain-based' learning. *School Science Review, 90*(330), 119–121.

Fisher, R. (2001). Philosophy in primary schools: Fostering thinking skills and literacy. *Reading, 35*(2), 67–73.

Goswami, U. (2004). Neuroscience and education: From research to practice? *National Review of Neuroscience, 7*(5), 406–413.

Higgins, S., Baumfield, V., & Hall, E. (2007). *Learning skills and the development of learning capabilities.* London: EPPI Centre, Social Science Research Unit, Institute of Education, University of London. Retrieved November 24 from http://eppi.ioe.ac.uk/cms/Default.aspx?tabid=1851.

Lipman, M. (1976). Philosophy for children. *Metaphilosophy, 7*(1), 17.

Lipman, M. (2003). *Thinking in education* (2nd ed.). New York: Cambridge University Press.

OECD (2007). *Understanding the brain: The birth of a learning science.* Paris: OECD.

Rowe, M. B. (1986). Wait time: Slowing down may be a way of speeding up! *Journal of Teacher Education, 37*(1), 43–50.

Shayer, M., & Adey, P. (2002). *Learning intelligence: Cognitive acceleration across the curriculum from 5 to 15 years*. Buckingham: Open University Press.

Smith, M. K., Wood, W. B., Adams, W. K., Wieman, C., Knight, J. K., Guild, N., & Su, T. T. (2009). Why peer discussion improves student performance on in-class concept questions. *Science, 323*(5910), 122–124.

Stephenson, J. (2009). Best practice? Advice provided to teachers about the use of Brain Gym® in Australian schools. *The Australian Journal of Education, 53*(2), 109–124.

Sylvan, L. J., & Christodoulou, J. A. (2010). Understanding the role of neuroscience in brain based products: A guide for educators and consumers. *Mind, Brain, and Education, 4*(1), 1–7.

CHAPTER ELEVEN
ICT IN THE SCIENCE CLASSROOM

Graham McMahon

OUTCOMES

By the end of this chapter you will be able to:

- Identify methods by which ICT can assist your classroom administration and teaching
- Evaluate your reasons for using ICT when teaching
- Use ICT to develop your students' higher order thinking skills

INTRODUCTION

> Inventions have long since reached their limit, and I see no hope for further developments. (Julius Sextus Frontinus, A.D. 10)

So said Julius Sextus Frontinus, a Roman engineer in the year A.D. 10. The past two thousand years have proved him a little off the mark. As I write this chapter, I am acutely aware that technology will have evolved further by the time this book is read. I will try to offer advice that will remain useful long after the next software suite is released and beyond the life of the current mobile phone.

This chapter begins with an overview of educational theory relevant to the use of information and communications technology (ICT) in science education, and you are encouraged to explore this theory further. The link between educational theory and the practicality of using computers in a science laboratory is developed. Computer use is then considered in terms of classroom administration, teaching and learning. Traps into which I have personally fallen will be addressed. References to specific software packages are minimised, but a table of useful websites is provided. Innovative approaches to ICT use in the classroom are explored through classroom snapshots.

EDUCATIONAL THEORY AND ICT

Passey (1999) argues that learning requires students to engage three cognitive operations: internalisation, internal processing and externalisation. As their names suggest, data enters the mind, is processed into new knowledge and is put to work. You may recognise some similarities with the input-process-output model used in computer programming. Chieu (2007) explains how this processing allows us to transfer skills from one area to another, while Jones and Spiro (1995) suggest that this is enhanced when using ICT, and it helps develop our higher order thinking.

In 1987 I replaced my handwritten marks book with a spreadsheet. Although primitive by today's standards, it sped up the administration of my lessons and the onerous task of assigning grades. I was doing nothing new, just faster and more accurately. In this respect, the software can be considered as a productivity tool—simply put, it made me more productive.

We can, however, do much more than increase productivity (Kirschner & Erkens, 2006). When the software basics have been mastered, we can apply them to higher order activities. Software used in this manner is referred to as a mindtool (Kirschner & Erkens, 2006). The difference between a productivity tool and mindtool can be explained as the difference between *doing things better* and *doing better things*. Computers allow us to do the following:

- *Cognitively amplify*. Software is used to perform tasks with greater accuracy and speed.
- *Share the work*. The computer performs calculations as required, stores the data and results, and formats the output. The user selects

the data for input, selects the processing of the data and analyses the results.

- *Generalise.* The same processes can be applied to different fields. Patterns from different domains can be observed.
- *Think critically.* Drawing on the previous point, links between constructs can be established and new knowledge created.
- *Conceptualise.* Parallel with the cognitive processes developed as the previous four points are instigated, methods of applying ICT and using it to reflect on new knowledge are forged.

The first and second feature describe lower order productivity tools. The remaining features address higher cognition and the theory of cognitive flexibility (Kirschner & Erkens, 2006). This serves as a reminder that both lower and higher order activities have their place in the science classroom. ICT applications allow you to develop higher cognition. In the science classroom, use software to increase productivity and develop your students' understanding of a given topic. This process will help develop students' cognitive skills, which can then be applied in other areas.

Probably the most compelling reason to use ICT in your science lessons is that, along with the microscope and Bunsen burner, the computer is a tool of science. By using it, you are modelling good scientific behaviour as well as helping your students.

CLASSROOM ADMINISTRATION AND ICT

I loosely define classroom administration as the activities that relate to teaching and learning, but that are not teaching or learning. This includes curriculum planning, lesson preparation, marking the roll and writing reports. It also includes handing out, collecting and marking assignments. It does not include tasks such as yard duty or supervising sports carnivals. In the previous section, I referred to using a spreadsheet as a grade book. This and other functions will be elaborated here.

Many educational systems allow you to lease or salary package a laptop computer. Others will provide one free for the term of your employment. If you are not within one of these systems, I encourage you to get your own computer. I have found that the two most versatile administration tools are the word processor and spreadsheet. While most schools will have access to commercial packages, you can perform equivalent functions with freeware or open source programs.

The word processor will let you create semester-long teaching programs. By setting up a template within a document, you can produce consistent-looking programs for each course. I find that it is easiest to lay out your work in a multi-columned table with your page in landscape format. This will allow you to quickly 'drag'n'drop' elements as you develop your teaching program. If you are required to produce formal lesson plans, you can achieve this in a similar way. Print yourself multiple copies—one to file in a hard-copy file, one to write notes on as your lessons progress and one for your supervisor. Make sure that you have your word processor set to the dictionary approved by your school administrators. If they require you to spell *recognise* as *recognize*, it is far easier to get it right at the beginning rather than constantly be editing your work. This is particularly true when preparing end-of-semester reports. (See Chapter 5 for more on planning for science teaching and learning.)

When preparing student reports, start early. Have your word processor running during class and jot down notes about each student. This helps you associate the right comments with the right student—a task that can be a little daunting in your first year of teaching. Use this document to edit your report comments before copying them to the official report. It is also useful to copy the comments into your marks book next to each student's name. Over the years you can look back over previous reports and comment on any improvements. It also reduces the likelihood of repeating the same comments.

Spreadsheets can perform a range of calculations far in excess of your needs. But they cannot do so without input from you. If you are not sure how to use built-in functions, or do not know how to create your own, I recommend that you search the internet for tutorials that will help you master the basics (and that is all that you need for a marks book). A useful starting point is <http://www.gcflearnfree.org>. Where possible, create your marks book before you begin the semester using a separate sheet for each class. Include all of the tasks that you will assess. Your marks book should be set up so that all you do is enter data; all the weighting and totalling of scores should be formula driven or you are wasting your time. Be prepared to overwrite any automatic grade allocation; there will be occasions that require you to modify the assessment profile of a student.

Many administrative tasks can be met by using a learning management system (LMS). Typical LMS functions include marking the roll, storing student marks, distributing and collecting assignments, and sharing tasks with other teachers. It is often possible to create auto-marking tests that allow student to monitor their own progress. While time is saved by distributing and collecting students' work, there are a few points to note. I use the manual distribution and collection time to 'eyeball' each student and exchange a few words with them, be this socially or curriculum related. I also use this time to quickly check the condition of the workbenches, gas taps, etc. as I move through the room. Automating these tasks does reduce the chances of students losing their work, and remote access to the system allows them to hand in work while not at school. You may find that there are restrictions on the types and sizes of files that may be transferred through an LMS. This can be addressed if you take the time to find out the limitations and your needs. If your school uses an LMS, find out how to use it effectively; your students will not be able to use it to submit their model solar houses!

When entering the Haiku Error Messages 21st Challenge, Dixon wrote: 'Three things are certain: Death, taxes, and lost data. Guess which has occurred' (Guillemets, 2012). You *will* lose your files. Make sure you have three copies of everything—all your worksheets, notes, lesson plans, teaching programs, student marks, everything. Keep a copy on your computer. Keep a copy on your server. Keep a copy on your thumb drive.

TEACHING SCIENCE WITH ICT

Teaching and learning science both involve theory and practical work. These elements can be enhanced by technology, although I believe that sensorimotor skills and conceptual understanding are best developed by manipulating real laboratory equipment. The US-based National Science Teacher Association (eScience Labs, 2008) suggests that the advantages of ICT become evident when the practical work:

- is too dangerous
- is too expensive
- requires equipment that is not available
- requires continuous monitoring

- extends beyond normal lesson time, or term time, or
- needs skills that the students have not yet developed.

If the students do not have the skills to perform the activity, you could also consider a teacher demonstration. This also applies to the first two points. I would like to add an extra 'drill and practice' use of ICT. Concepts that have been addressed through practical work can be enhanced if that practical work can be duplicated. Software simulations allow activities to be repeated in the school library or at home.

Hennessy et al. (2007) explain that computer simulations allow students to explore 'what if?' questions in relative safety. While this may appear to be 'off-task' behaviour, it promotes creative thinking and can lead to a broader understanding of a given topic. They caution that it may reinforce alternative conceptions should the results not coincide with what was expected, and recommend that any such conflicts are addressed.

Probably the most frequent use of ICT for teaching is the delivery of 'notes' via computer and projector. This really should be considered an entry-level use of ICT; it is barely removed from writing notes on the blackboard while students laboriously copy them down, reinforcing the erroneous 'empty vessel' perspective of students explained more fully in Chapter 2. When using a computer and projector, make use of the multimedia capabilities. Short animations made with software such as Adobe Flash™ can be used to demonstrate molecular-level activity, solar and lunar eclipses or tectonic plate movement, to name a few. Examples can be found via the web links listed in Table 11.1.

Tablet PCs allow you to draw freehand on a computer screen in much the same way as you would on a whiteboard. The advantage of this is that you are facing the class, confident that what you see on your screen is visible to all of your students. You are not blocking their view, and by facing them you can gauge their level of understanding as well as keeping an eye on the back row! If you are fortunate enough to have a wireless connection in your classroom, you can move around the room at the same time.

The gradual replacement of VHS video with DVD allows the use of these materials in the classroom to be modified. Typically, a video tape will have a worksheet. Students complete the exercises as the information is presented or when the video has finished. Those who complete it while viewing need to stop viewing as they record their answers and consequently miss sections of the video. Others may miss

TABLE 11.1: Useful websites for science teaching

Title/topic	URL	Comments
YouTube™	www.youtube.com	Great for getting motivational clips, introductions to topics etc. Have a listen to <http://www.youtube.com/watch?v=jJvAL-iiLnQ> and <http://www.youtube.com/watch?v=C1_uez5WX1o&feature=related>.
TeacherTube™	www1.teachertube.com/	Like YouTube™ but aimed at teachers. Do a search for 'Ten Things You Do Not Learn About Teaching in College'.
WebQuests	http://webquest.org/index.php	A useful one-stop shop for finding webquests.
Using multimedia	http://ascilite.org.au/ajet/ajet21/chambers.html	The name says it all.
Planet Oit	http://oit.cs.ndsu.nodak.edu/menu	Very good geology program for Years 8–10, especially for those who enjoy simulation games.
Murder under the microscope	www.microscope.edu.au/	Very good for secondary school environmental science. Promotes cooperative group work, problem-solving and environmental management.
Questacon	http://canberra.questacon.edu.au/	Australia's national science museum. As well as general museum information, this site has some innovative 'games' to teach science concepts.
The Learning Federation	www.thelearningfederation.edu.au/	An Australian-based collection of digital curriculum resources.
Molecular Workbench	http://mw.concord.org/modeler/	A collection of useful simulations, with the ability to add your own.
Education Services Australia	http://www.esa.edu.au	A comprehensive website of Australian curriculum and assessment resources.

important points and cannot individually rewind the tape. This is compounded if the video is viewed before starting the written exercises. There are systems available that allow a DVD to be played via a file server to individual students' computers. This gives control of the video to each student. They are able to stop, start or replay sections as they need without disrupting their peers. Headphones are essential, and while many students have their own it is a good idea to have a class set available. You will also need to closely monitor what the students are viewing.

Many of us have attended seminars that begin with the presenter struggling to get the computer equipment to work. Reasons for this problem fall into two broad groups: user error and equipment error. If you will be using computer equipment in a classroom, make sure you have practised with it beforehand. Ensure that everything plugs together and has power, that loudspeakers work and so on. If necessary, enlist the help of a colleague or laboratory technician. Once you have set up the equipment, move around the room so that you can view it from different angles. Make sure that the screen is not washed out by excessive light; check that the volume is audible.

Equipment occasionally will fail to work and technical support will not always be available. You can waste precious class time and risk your students engaging in off-task behaviour as you try to fix a malfunction. It is a good idea to have a back-up for your lesson that will achieve the planned objectives.

Does your science department have computers within its laboratories? You may need to engage in a little room-swapping with your colleagues to gain access to ICT. If your school has its computers organised into specific computer rooms, you will need to book your access—often weeks in advance. Computer classes will have been timetabled during the previous year and all other subjects will vie for the remaining free periods. You may also want to check that the infrastructure is capable of running the software you require.

LEARNING SCIENCE WITH ICT

The author Norman Douglas (1868–1952) once wrote: 'If you want to see what children can do, you must stop giving them things' (Douglas, in Bagley, 2008). Douglas's comment suggests that children's creative thinking can be developed via simple play rather than swamping them with toys. A modern-day version could be: 'If you want to see what children can do, give them a computer.' In doing so, you give them access to infinite possibilities via the internet: socialising, creative programming and the application of ICT to learning science. Bear in mind, however, that if you choose to use ICT within your lessons it should relate directly to your lesson objectives and enhance your students' learning.

ICT can be used as an alternative to laboratory work, for example, by using computer simulations of experiments. Another useful approach is to integrate ICT with the existing practical activities. Figure 11.1 shows examples of types of ICT that can be utilised by students at different stages of the scientific method. For example, data logging, digital images and digital video can be used by students during the conduct phase of an experiment or investigation to support data collection.

Within science, ICT can be used as both a productivity tool and mindtool. Spreadsheets can be used when analysing and graphing numerical data. Sliders within spreadsheets allow students to quickly test the relationships between variables. The frequently asked question 'Please sir, what type of graph should I use?' is usually answered with 'The one that best explains your data.' Spreadsheets permit the almost instantaneous reproduction of the same data in different graph types.

The nature of the World Wide Web makes it quite easy for students to simply copy and paste answers to assignments without internalising any information. I suggest that the real fault lies in the nature of the assignment. If an assignment question requires a short response, it will encourage copy/pasting and rote learning. For example, the question 'What is transpiration?' will encourage students to simply enter 'define: transpiration' into their search engine and then copy one of the 29 500 results.

Snapshots 11.1, 11.2 and 11.3 demonstrate the use of ICT in science. The emphasis is on students' learning rather than the teacher's teaching. These snapshots show the use of ICT at different levels; while you could simply adopt these for yourself, also consider other ways in which your students could use ICT in your classroom. An excellent starting point for ideas is the World Wide Web. A search for *science education* and *ICT* in December 2011 resulted in more than 33 million links. While many of these will have been removed by the time you are reading this chapter, others will have been created. Table 11.1 (above) describes some sites that have remained active for several years.

FIGURE 11.1: Uses of ICT at different stages of the scientific method

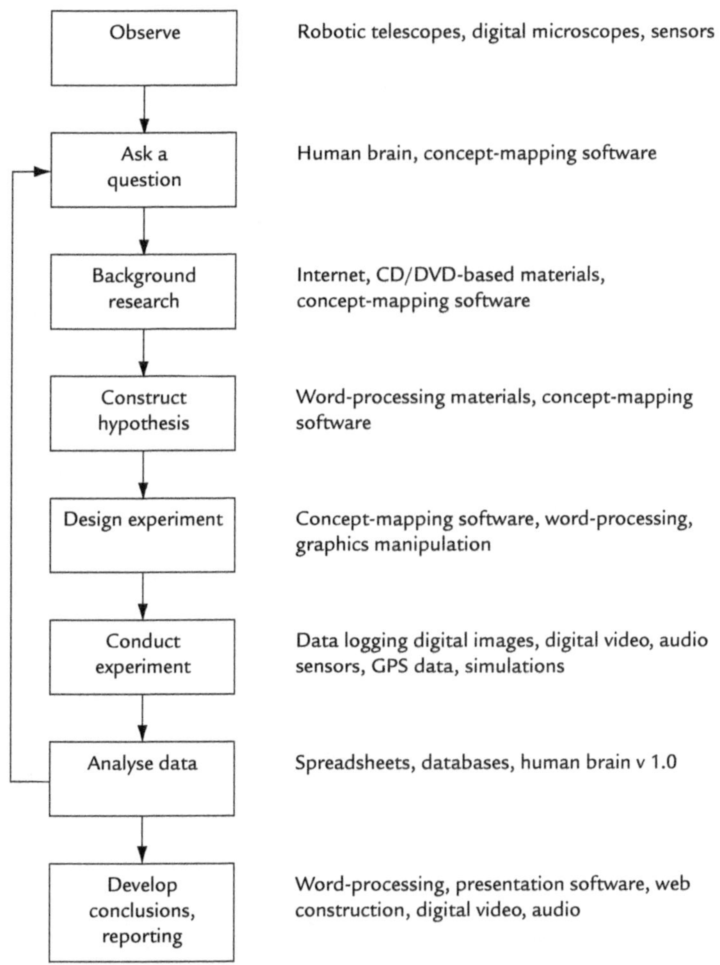

SNAPSHOT 11.1: Extreme sports in space

Peta was timetabled to teach a Year 10 astronomy class. This was being run as an alternative to a more advanced physics class—the students were of average to below-average ability with mixed levels of motivation. Peta also taught a number of these students in an ICT class, in which students were developing image-editing skills. One of the objectives of the astronomy class was for students to amass knowledge about the planets in our solar system—size, distance from the sun, key features and so on. The usual assignment required students to conduct library research on a given planet and in a final lesson compile a summary table by collecting data from other students. Peta was unsure how well this task would succeed, given that most of the data could be copied from the internet with little internalisation.

With the approval of her head of department, Peta revised the assignment. Students had to incorporate the required data into a travel poster advertising 'Extreme Sports in Space'. While the posters were marked according to their scientific accuracy and not artistic ability, students in her ICT class could submit the same poster for their ICT image editing assignment. According to Peta, the most noticeable difference was the enthusiasm with which her students approached the assignment. Final posters advertised mountain climbing on Mars, cruising the methane oceans of Titan and hang-gliding in 2000 km/hr winds on Saturn.

SNAPSHOT 11.2: Gravity of the situation

Stefan had been helping his Year 7 students develop scientific inquiry skills using the Predict-Observe-Explain technique (see Chapter 3 for more about POE). His students had designed experiments to test the idea that heavier objects fall faster than light objects. With the students having completed the experimental design and conducted their tests, Stefan wanted to use their work in a writing skills exercise. At a recent ICT seminar, Stefan had been introduced to the software Rationale™—a program designed to help develop critical thinking. This package allows students to sort and structure their ideas in a series of boxes, with questions to prompt them, shown in the screenshot below.

Stefan found that by using Rationale™, his students could turn their work into a colour-coded text file that could be edited further with word processing software. All of his students seemed to appreciate their ideas 'magically' turning into a written report. In particular, the less able students were not faced with a blank sheet and the daunting question, 'What do I write?' More advanced students recognised that they could improve their report by editing the document.

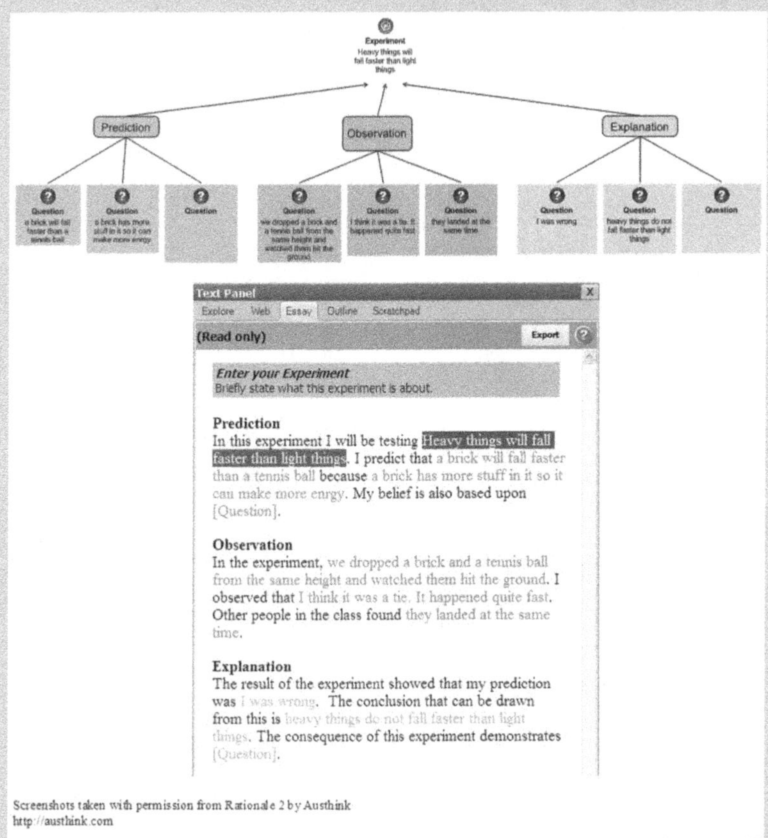

Screenshots taken with permission from Rationale 2 by Austhink
http://austhink.com

A screenshot of a completed Predict-Observe-Explain template and the automatically generated essay structure

SNAPSHOT 11.3: Circuit training

Michelle had been teaching science for ten years. At one school, she was timetabled to teach a unit in electricity for Year 9 students. While the students were quite enthusiastic about the practical activities, they were less inclined to absorb themselves in the theory that they were required to master. The previous year, Michelle's science department had bought the Crocodile Clips suite of software, which enables circuits to be designed and tested on the computer screen prior to actually building them. Michelle created a series of theory puzzles to be completed as an introduction to the laboratory work. An example is shown in the screenshot below. By using the computers, the students perceived the task to be more of a hands-on practical session rather than 'boring theory'.

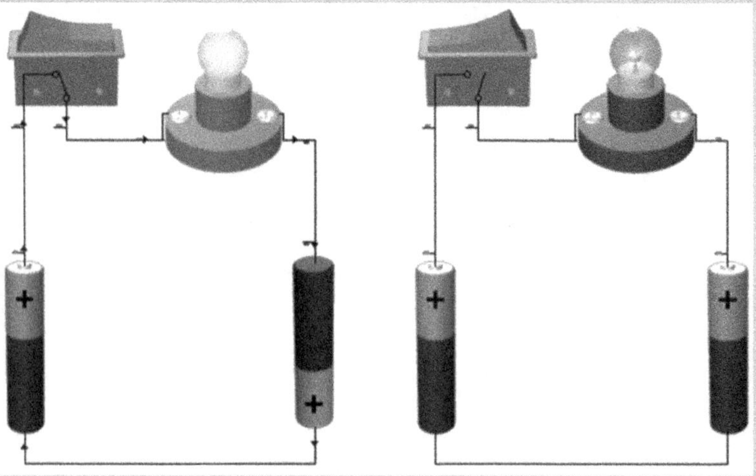

1. Build the two circuits shown above. Which circuit do you think will work?
2. List and explain your reasons why one circuit will not work.

Source: Screenshots taken with permission from Crocodile Clips Ltd, www.yenka.com.

While search engines have made it easy for students to answer their set assignments without really internalising anything, they can be used to create tasks that will challenge your students. Your assignment can be designed as a WebQuest. WebQuests are inquiry-based tasks, usually attempted in groups, that require students to use information rather than simply find it. You provide the websites (or any other appropriate resources) that you want your students to use. A properly constructed WebQuest will help your students to develop critical thinking rather than simple knowledge recall. If you are unfamiliar with WebQuests, use your search engine to search for 'What is a WebQuest'. You also might like to search for 'How to search with Google' to help you effectively find web resources.

A FEW CAVEATS

You will need to consider issues regarding access to the hardware and software. If computers are used within the science classroom, what is their proximity to additional equipment, liquids, and other features unique to a laboratory that may be dangerous? Reinforcing laboratory safety rules should occur at the start of and during the lesson. Watch out for students who dominate the computer. You could consider rostering group members through distinct roles such as Group Leader, Experimenter and Data Entry Operator. This will also help address the inevitable situation in which a student has been denied access to the computer system (for disciplinary reasons) or the new student who has yet to be given their own workspace or password.

Computers have been used within science classrooms since the late 1970s, and should be considered part of your normal laboratory equipment. You will find them invaluable for administration, teaching and learning. While they are no longer a novelty in schools, computers do still have a strong, motivational influence for most students. However, not all students are computer gurus; their degree of computer literacy could affect their science learning. A lack of competence or confidence with computers could appear as disinterest that results in off-task behaviour. Consider discussing their computing skills with the school's ICT staff when deciding whether your planned activity will be suitable. All this takes effort; you may even wonder whether it is worth the trouble. However, Rogers and Finlayson (2003) demonstrated that the integration of ICT with science enhanced the learning experience, and the teachers they surveyed claimed that using ICT helped to achieve the learning objectives in 92 per cent of their lessons. Remember that the computer is a powerful tool, but only *one* tool. Do not overlook how your own personality, enthusiasm and knowledge will influence your students' learning.

SUMMARY OF KEY POINTS

The prudent use of ICT in science can help students develop higher order thinking skills; learning is achieved through active engagement rather than by passive observation. ICT allows the active engagement with all areas of science. In addition to assisting with routine, lower levels of a given subject, ICT allows our students become equipped to test the question 'I wonder what happens if . . . ?'

DISCUSSION QUESTIONS

11.1 Figure 11.1 shows types of software that can be used during practical work. How many other uses can you add?

11.2 Which of these uses are best described as productivity tools? mind tools? Which are more important?

11.3 The use of mobile phones is banned in some schools. Should students be allowed to use mobile phones for data collection, storage and transmission in science? What are the potential problems with this approach and how can the problems be addressed?

11.4 Do you believe that you have the necessary skills to use computers effectively in the classroom? What are your strengths and weaknesses with regard to ICT use and how could you improve?

REFERENCES

Bagley, E. (2008). *Catholic education: Thoughts about children and facts about Catholic education outcomes—part 3*. Retrieved 24 November 2011 from http://ezinearticles.com/?Catholic-Education---Thoughts-About-Children-and-Facts-About-Catholic-Education-Outcomes---Part-3&id=1005041.

Chieu, V. M. (2007). An operational approach for building learning environments supporting cognitive flexibility. *Educational Technology and Society*, *10*(3), 32–46.

eScience Labs, Inc. (2008). *The use of computers in science education*. Retrieved 24 November 2011 from http://www.esciencelabs.com/news/2008/01/the_use_computers_science_education.

Guillemets, T. (2012). *The Quote Garden*. Retrieved 2 May 2012 from www.quotegarden.com.

Hennessy, S., Wishart, J., Whitelock, D., Deaney, R., Brawn, R., la Velle, L., McFarlane, A., Ruthven, K., & Winterbottom, M. (2007). Pedagogical approaches for technology-integrated science teaching. *Computers and Education*, *48*, 137–152.

Jones, R. A., & Spiro, R. J. (1995). Contextualization, cognitive flexibility, and hypertext: The convergence of interpretive theory, cognitive psychology, and advanced information technologies. In S. L. Star (Ed.), *The cultures of computing*. Oxford: Blackwell.

Kirschner, P. A., & Erkens, G. (2006). Cognitive tools and mindtools for collaborative learning. *Journal of Educational Computing Research*, *35*(2), 199–209.

Passey, D. (1999). *Higher order thinking skills: An exploration of aspects of learning and thinking and how ICT can be used to support these processes*. Retrieved 24 November 2011 from http://www.northerngrid.org/ngflwebsite/hots/HOTSintro.pdf.

Rogers, L., & Finlayson, H. (2003). Does ICT work in the classroom? Part 1: The individual teacher experience. *School Science Review*, *84*(309), 105–112.

CHAPTER TWELVE

EQUITY AND EXCELLENCE IN THE SCIENCE CURRICULUM

Léonie J. Rennie

OUTCOMES

By the end of this chapter you will be able to:

- Discuss the meaning of equity in science education
- Describe what is meant by equity and excellence in the science curriculum
- Suggest a range of equitable teaching and assessment strategies for the science classroom

INTRODUCTION

Teacher 1: This school has always had a social justice policy, ever since I have been here. In fact we're trailblazers in that regard.

Léonie: What indicated to you that this school has a policy?

Teacher 1: You only have to walk into the school to see that there is an imbalance of boys to girls and there's a whole heap of ethnic kids; that there's kids that are dressed badly and kids that are really rich. I mean, that's the kind of school that it is. The kids from [an affluent suburb] are wealthy. It's not unusual for a kid to talk about getting $100 pocket money a week for doing nothing. And in the same class some of the kids from [a poor suburb] have never had pocket money in their lives. So, the problems were there. We had to cope with them. The school goes out of its way to make sure that problems don't arise . . . I don't know if we have written policies, probably not, but if you look at the amount of fighting that takes place in the school, there's far less than almost any other school I have been in, yet there are all the ingredients for a disaster here.

Teacher 2: I see the big ESL [English as a Second Language] population as a bonus to the school more than anything else. The Caucasians get to see that the Asians and others are just normal sorts of kids. I've been in other situations where that's not the case. We hardly have any instances of name-calling and fights. We do have something occasionally but it's usually something other than a racial problem that starts it off. I think it makes the kids more tolerant.

Teacher 3: I don't think we have a gender policy in the school that's been written down. Staff support gender equality and equity issues in the school, mainly because there are equity issues with race and culture in the school. There are so many different cultural backgrounds, students from [an institution for troubled adolescents] with emotional problems, some handicapped students, yet no one seems to mind.

Teacher 4: Although we did have one student recently who was dressed in a gothic style and was considered strange by her peers. Somehow she got suspended and left because she thought she had been unfairly treated. I don't know what happened but I was very disappointed. She was the best art student I have ever had, really brilliant, and I was looking forward to her doing art for a long time. Having taught gifted students, I think she was gifted but not recognised, and sometimes they have difficulty fitting in.

This chapter is about equity. In the discussion above, compiled from interviews with teachers at City High School (a pseudonym), social justice, equality and equity were three terms teachers used in their discussion about coping with the very diverse population of their school. These terms all refer to how people are treated and whether they get what Australians call 'a fair go'. These teachers perceived their school to have an integrated and tolerant body of teachers and students and, perhaps except for the gifted art student, people received a fair go. But as other teachers said:

> *Teacher 5:* I think the good integration just doesn't happen by itself. I think the ESL people have got a very close eye on it. They help kids in many ways, working through their problems.
>
> *Teacher 6:* It is a credit to the staff here that the school is not disrupted. If anyone were to be singled out, it would be the ESL department, they do a superb job of counselling and talking to kids, even those who are now in the mainstream keep going back to them. The year coordinators also do their duty over and above what is required and play a large role in the school. The Student Services Committee is also important in keeping the school working smoothly.

Clearly, having a 'school working smoothly', an equitable school, takes constant effort and a good deal of pastoral care. It also requires giving careful thought to the curriculum. What does equity mean for us as teachers concerned with the science curriculum that is offered in our classrooms? Does an equitable science curriculum mean that all students are treated equally? Does it mean that they have equal access to learning opportunities? Does equity refer to equal educational outcomes at the end, or does it mean something else altogether? It is worth exploring these different meanings of equity to understand how we can work towards the best outcomes for our students.

WHAT DOES IT MEAN TO TREAT STUDENTS EQUALLY?

Treating students equally should be fundamental to equitable educational practice. In the science classroom, equal treatment means that all students receive exactly the same curriculum, the same instruction from the teacher, the same resources to work with and the same assessment tasks to demonstrate their learning. But all students are not the same. The teachers' comments above demonstrate that students have very different background experiences (often associated with socio-cultural variables such as their ethnicity, social class and gender). They also have different interests, expectations and learning styles. These differences mean that students differ in their preparedness to benefit from the science curriculum, so if they all receive the same instruction some will learn better than others, and be advantaged, and some will learn less well than others, and be disadvantaged. Two examples will make this clear.

Suppose the science instruction uses the textbook as the central learning resource. Very likely poor readers will be disadvantaged and may make less progress than good readers. Addressing this disadvantage means giving help to poor readers so that they can use the textbook more effectively. Suppose students are given an assignment requiring the use of resources at home, such as the internet or making observations of plants in a garden. Some students may be disadvantaged because they do not have access to these things at home. Such students will need assistance to do their homework assignment. They may need time to use the internet in the school library, for example, or help to arrange access to a garden. Thus we see that treating all students in the same way invariably leads to disadvantage for some students. Overcoming the disadvantage usually means treating students unequally!

WHAT DOES IT MEAN TO GIVE STUDENTS EQUAL ACCESS TO LEARNING OPPORTUNITIES?

Giving students equal access to learning opportunities means that, if they so choose, they can all participate fully in the science activities and assessment tasks that make up the science curriculum. This means that how we teach, the pedagogical and assessment approaches we use, must be varied to accommodate differences in students' interests, backgrounds and experiences. In other words, students are given instructional cues that they can understand, and assessment tasks that enable them all to demonstrate what they have learned and can do.

To continue the earlier examples, the poor readers would benefit from instructional cues other than the written words in the textbook. Providing a choice of science homework assignments might sidestep the problem for students without internet access or a garden at home. Alternatively, regular visits to the library or into the school grounds would give students choices about where and how to tackle their assignments. Giving students equal opportunities to participate in the science curriculum means ensuring that, overall, the teaching methods, resources and assessments provide a variety of instructional alternatives suited to the range of students' experiences and situations.

WHAT DOES IT MEAN FOR STUDENTS TO HAVE EQUAL EDUCATIONAL OUTCOMES?

Having equal educational outcomes means that, in the end, all students will possess the same knowledge, skills and attitudes about science. But achieving equal educational outcomes in terms of marks doesn't mean that students have all learned the same things. Students arrive in their science class with different patterns of background knowledge, skills and ideas. If the outcomes are similar at the end, it usually means that students have learned different things. Think of it this way: if students are all to finish at the same place but have different starting points, then they will have to take different paths to get there. Some paths might be short and others long; some might be difficult and others easy. If we want all students to achieve the desired educational outcomes of the science curriculum, we will have to allow for these different paths by offering science instruction with sufficient variety to accommodate the needs of different students. Students have different levels of interest, motivation and persistence, and they may not all want to achieve to the same level. However, an equitable science curriculum will give them the best chance of achieving well and to the best of their ability.

EQUITY AND EXCELLENCE IN THE SCIENCE CURRICULUM

'Australian schooling promotes equity and excellence' (MCEETYA, 2008, p. 7). This is the first of two educational goals for young Australians agreed by all Australian education ministers in December 2008. The *Melbourne Declaration* stated that all Australian governments and all school sectors must:

- provide all students with access to high-quality schooling that is free from discrimination based on gender, language, sexual orientation, pregnancy, culture, ethnicity, religion, health or disability, socio-economic background or geographic location
- ensure that schools build on local cultural knowledge and experience of Indigenous students as a foundation for learning, and work in partnership with local communities on all aspects of the schooling process, including to promote high expectations for the learning outcomes of Indigenous students. (2008, p. 7)

Other paragraphs refer to the need to ensure that sources of disadvantage, such as homelessness, refugee status and remoteness, cease to be significant determinants of educational outcomes. The Australian Curriculum Assessment and Reporting Authority (ACARA), in the context of the *Melbourne Declaration*, discussed the diversity of learners and stated that its curricula would be inclusive of all students.

In our earlier discussion, we saw that an acceptable meaning of equity in science teaching and learning is that no student suffers disadvantage from the way the science curriculum is enacted in the classroom. An equitable and excellent science curriculum, then, is one in which both the content and the pedagogy are inclusive of all students, enabling them to participate in ways that are appropriate for them and thus have the best chance of achieving the desired educational outcomes at the end.

We can distinguish three important components of an equitable science curriculum. First, all students have access to a wide range of science-related knowledge, skills and values. Second, students' different starting points, learning styles and backgrounds are accommodated. Third, students are given opportunities to think about science, its culture and the people who do science. Let us examine each of these components in more detail.

ACCESS TO APPROPRIATE SCIENCE-RELATED KNOWLEDGE, SKILLS AND VALUES

Access is a significant word in this first component of an equitable curriculum. Providing access means that students are able to understand and make use of the science-related knowledge, skills and values, otherwise there can be no empowering. Simply putting knowledge in front of students isn't enough; it must be meaningful and relevant to them.

In preparing their report for the Australian government, Goodrum, Hackling and Rennie (2001) surveyed over 4000 science students Australia wide. Students wrote about the things they liked, the things they didn't like and how they thought their science class could be improved so they could learn more. Some students' comments appear in Snapshot 12.1. My continuing conversations with students indicates little change in their views.

SNAPSHOT 12.1: Students' comments about science at school (indicating year level and sex; b = boy, g = girl)

What are the things that you really like about science in your class?

- The way that we can have class discussions and talk about things that aren't actually in the things that we study but are relevant and matter to us. (10g)
- Our teacher explains things really clearly in a way we can understand/relate to. We get hands-on experience by doing experiments. I learn things that have something to do with the career I want to follow. (10g)
- That it is a small class, which means you get more attention. (8b)
- I enjoy learning about the things I am curious about, yet often I find myself wondering about the point of some of the things we learn. (11g)
- I enjoy the discussions held and the ability for everyone to voice their opinion. (10b)
- Practical exercise when you get to use your hands and imagination. (7b)

What are the things that you don't like about science in your class?

- We don't get to do experiments as often as I would like to. Sometimes we learn things that we probably won't need to know later in life. (10g)
- It is sometimes hard to get help without being noticed. (10b)
- I don't like it that the chapter 'How life begins' is all based on girl stuff. It is victimisation and sexist. (8g)
- Sometimes the teacher talks too fast and I couldn't understand. (10g)
- We don't get to do enough pracs and have to copy pages of notes from the board and in the process get bored and lose interest in our work. (9b)
- Taking notes. Repeatedly going over things I understood the first time. (9b)

How could your science class be improved so that you could learn more?

- I think we should focus on less areas and cover them more comprehensively. (9b)

- More experiments. Work with computers. More practical work—for example, outside, at the zoo. (10g)
- Interact more, as opposed to just listening to the teacher talk/copy notes off the board. (10g)
- Have a kinder teacher who explains things better. Have less homework that is meaningless. (8b)
- Learn about engines and cars (practical work). (9g)
- Maybe more guest speakers. I am a visual person so I learn more from videos. (9g)
- Maybe some more hands-on stuff, more getting in and physically doing pracs, not just writing about it. It's fun putting theory into practice. (11b)

Students like to deal with information they find relevant and meaningful, and to discuss it with others so it makes sense to them. This helps to make science accessible. Not surprisingly, students get bored copying notes, doing exercises from the textbook and listening to constant teacher talk. It seems that science becomes less accessible through the passive routines of writing, listening and doing work students find meaningless. Students like variety because it maintains their interest and provides different ways to access knowledge and skills. Many students wrote about getting out of the classroom and using other resources, like the Year 9 girl who liked guest speakers and videos because she was 'a visual person'. Variety enables those less interested or able in science to find a way to connect with and participate in science. Variety helps take account of the diversity among students, and increases access to the knowledge, skills and values offered in the science curriculum. (See Chapter 9 for more about student engagement in science lessons.)

RECOGNISING AND ACCOMMODATING DIVERSITY

The equitable science curriculum accommodates students' different starting points, learning styles and background experiences. Recognising and respecting diversity among students requires diversity in the kinds of instruction, resources and assessment tasks that students are offered, and also diversity in the selection and presentation of the science content. This means recognising, valuing and including the understandings and knowledge of all groups, particularly those in the minority.

In Snapshot 12.1, one comment came from a boy who found it 'hard to get help without being noticed', and another from a girl whose teacher talked too fast. To include each of these students fully in classroom activities, the teacher would need to be aware of these potential problems and take steps to accommodate them, checking the boy's progress unobtrusively, perhaps, and being sensitive to the girl's ability to comprehend what is being said. While the boy's problem might be attributable to self-consciousness, a personal issue, it is possible that the girl experienced difficulty because English was not her first language. This draws attention to an important issue: sometimes being a member of a minority group—such as migrants or Indigenous students, who often have English as a second language—can be the basis of systematic (albeit unintentional) exclusion from participation in the science curriculum.

Read Snapshot 12.2, which records part of a conversation with some Year 9 girls from a class of mostly boys. Three of the four girls are feeling left out of the classroom conversation, and they believe it affects their work and grades.

Re-read the conversation among teachers that opened this chapter and see how teachers categorised students into different socio-cultural groups. They referred to boys and girls, ethnic kids, ESL population, Caucasians and Asians, kids with emotional problems, handicapped students and gifted students. These teachers emphasised the diversity of students and their needs, and the effort required to keep the school working smoothly. We tend to have different expectations about people from different socio-cultural groups, and this alerts us to issues such as new English speakers needing help to deal with spoken and written English. But we must be careful not to fall into the trap of treating students according to stereotypes based upon their membership of particular socio-cultural sub-groups. For example, we often have inappropriate expectations, based on gender stereotypes, about what boys and girls are interested in and how they should behave. Look again at Snapshot 12.2. Stereotypically, it is males rather than females who are interested in cars, but Julie knew about cars. Further, in Snapshot 12.1, it was another Year 9 girl, not a boy, who wanted to learn about engines and cars. While many girls (and possibly some boys) might feel left out of a discussion about cars, some don't. It is not a good solution to avoid talking about cars; a better solution is to use a variety

SNAPSHOT 12.2: Students discuss feelings of being excluded in classroom conversation (names are pseudonyms)

Jill: The guys all talk about something and you just sit there, and they say don't you know this? Don't you know this?

Michelle: They always talk about cars! As if you'd know about cars!

Julie: I do!

Michelle: Yeah, you do!

Léonie: Do the teachers or the boys talk about cars?

Annette: Yeah, sometimes the teacher talks with the guys—but then he sort of leaves out the girls, you know?

Jill, Michelle: Yes.

Annette: You know what I mean?

Léonie: Do you think that gets reflected in your marks at all? Your grades?

Annette: Yes, it does. Like, when you go home to do homework, you sort of think I just hate that teacher so much, so you just try to forget the subject altogether and that affects it, you don't feel like doing the work.

Jill: You don't feel like going to class.

Annette: You just feel like *dying* in the classroom!

of real-world examples so that all students experience meaningful illustrations to help their understanding.

There is an important message here: inequity arises when students are treated according to stereotypes based upon their membership of particular socio-cultural sub-groups. It is more equitable to treat students according to their individual needs.

OPPORTUNITIES TO EXAMINE SCIENCE AND ITS CULTURE

The Australian science curriculum strand Science as a Human Endeavour emphasises that science is a social construction. Humans build knowledge and understanding from observations and experiment, and rebuild that knowledge when new evidence becomes available. Not surprisingly, different cultures build different explanations of natural phenomena. For example, Western science, with its Eurocentric roots, discusses climate in terms of four seasons, whereas Indigenous communities may work with two to six seasons, depending on their geographic location in Australia. Exploring these different ways of dealing with environmental knowledge can be the basis of inclusive classroom activities that illuminate this strand of science.

Science has not always been a school subject available to every young person at school. Early in the twentieth century in many Australian schools, girls did extra sewing classes while boys did science! Later, when science became available to all students—some of whom did not learn successfully—socio-cultural issues such as gender, race and class were perceived to be affecting the learning of certain groups of students. Researchers argued that science in schools and in the wider society was presented culturally as male, white, Western and middle class (Parker, Rennie & Fraser, 1996). Thus the content and practice of science served to maintain the interests and values of these dominant groups, both inside and outside schools, excluding other groups. Various approaches were taken to remedy this. Textbooks using sexist or racist language, or depicting mainly white, Western males doing science, for example, were discarded as more inclusive resources became available. However, ensuring equity means doing more than this. It requires an active examination of how science and science education work to value and position one group over another—middle class over working class, for example, or being more welcoming of males than of females. This perspective (sometimes called a socially critical perspective) means more than adapting the science content and instruction to be inclusive of students' gender and culture, attitudes and beliefs. It means that offering an equitable science education requires accepting some responsibility for challenging the traditional representations of science and the science curriculum, even if that challenge makes some people a bit uncomfortable. We need to actively examine the ways the nature of science generally and science in schools in particular is

structured to ensure that we are not unintentionally excluding some students.

Stereotyped attitudes still exist about who should, and can, do science. Science and mathematics are highly regarded in the workplace by tertiary institutions and by parents as passports to better jobs. Tertiary entrance subjects are accorded higher esteem than school-assessed subjects. Students and their parents know this and, despite the best efforts by teachers at City High School to advise students to enrol in science subjects compatible with their ability, there were often large enrolments of students in physics and chemistry who had unrealistic expectations. The teachers' perceptions about students' choice of subjects discussed in Snapshot 12.3 indicate a belief that more boys than girls made unwise subject choices, and the net result of gender-based social pressures was perceived by many teachers to be problematic—too many boys in physics and chemistry and too few girls.

Equity in science teaching and learning, and an excellent science curriculum, mean that all students, regardless of their socio-cultural group, can choose science and a science career if they wish. But this may require rethinking the traditional ways we teach science. City High School science staff were restructuring the science curriculum to include more technological applications to increase its relevance to students. Here is one teacher's view:

> The problem is with the subject. Being involved with things like the technology program, explaining what needed to be done with the subject, you keep coming back to the issue that the subject itself, the way we teach it, needs to change. We weren't focusing on girls, we were focusing just on relevance and making people more interested in the subject for both boys and girls. We came up with things like the subject needs to be more supportive, it needs to be less competitive, it needs to engage skills other than just figuring out a right answer to a problem and putting your hand up, it needs to have people working in groups because that's how people work in real life—communicating, waiting, talking, disagreeing, making mistakes, learning . . . So for me the change is going to come around by the way we teach—more group work, more cooperation, more things shared and written down and less of the teacher out the front in control.

SNAPSHOT 12.3: Teachers' views of social expectations and science subject choice

Science teacher: I am concerned that we have three physics classes scheduled for Year 11 next year and the smallest is 24 students. It's one of the hardest subjects and many won't be able to cope. The physics teacher is depressed because half of his Year 10 class failed the final exam—not very rewarding for a teacher. General science [school-assessed subject] is offered but doesn't run because there are not enough takers.

English teacher 1: Kids choose subjects for socially motivated reasons, I think. Like 'I must do top-level maths because they are the hardest subjects so if I do them—even if I don't pass them—I am better.' 'I want to be a doctor even though I'm failing every subject so I must do top maths.' I don't think it is a gendered thing, it's a goal-oriented thing—their perceptions of what is socially acceptable.

English teacher 2: Just as the other way they don't want to do 'vegie' maths or 'vegie' English. It doesn't matter what sex they are, it's whether they perceive themselves as capable or intelligent or incapable and 'vegie'.

English teacher 1: Boys are choosing subjects that they can see they can get more jobs with, more with maths and science than they can with social science. They say to me, 'Why do you teach English when you've done maths and science?' It's like obviously you've chosen second best if you could do the others. There is still that maths/science push for them.

SUMMARY OF KEY POINTS

To ensure that girls and boys from every socio-cultural group can succeed at science, we need a science curriculum that promotes instructional, pedagogical and assessment strategies that are inclusive of all students, and that also engages with the human aspects relating to the nature of science and the science curriculum. An equitable approach to science means accepting students as they are, and building on their interests, experiences and learning styles, instead of trying to make them fit some stereotype of what is a 'good' science student.

Some important points from this chapter include the following:

- Equity and excellence in science teaching and learning mean that no student is disadvantaged by the science curriculum or the way that curriculum is enacted in the classroom.
- Some students, for personal reasons or because of stereotyping about their social group, are at risk of exclusion from participating in science.
- An equitable science curriculum:
  - provides all students with access to a wide and empowering range of knowledge, skills and values
  - recognises and accommodates students' different starting points, learning styles and previous experiences
  - values and includes the understandings and knowledge of all groups, and
  - provides opportunities for students to think about science, its culture and the people who do science.
- Ensuring that all students can succeed in science may require rethinking the traditional ways of teaching and learning science.

DISCUSSION QUESTIONS

12.1 How would you structure a science topic on weather that dealt with both Western and Indigenous knowledge? (The Bureau of Meteorology website on Indigenous weather knowledge may help your planning: see <www.bom.gov.au/iwk/about/index.shtml>.)

12.2 During the 1980s, considerable attention was given to preparing resources for science teaching that were 'gender inclusive'. Teachers found that such resources were excellent for teaching other socio-cultural groups, especially those based on ethnicity and class. Why do you think that might be? (The August 1989 issue of *The Australian Science Teachers Journal*, devoted to gender-inclusive strategies, will be helpful.)

12.3 Select a current, controversial socioscientific issue and find several media articles offering different viewpoints. Describe how you would approach a class discussion of this issue in ways that would include all of the students in your classroom.

REFERENCES

Goodrum, D., Hackling, M., & Rennie, L. (2001). *The status and quality of teaching and learning of science in Australian schools: A research report.* Canberra: Department of Education, Training and Youth Affairs.

MCEETYA (2008). *The Melbourne Declaration on Educational Goals for Young Australians.* Canberra: Author.

Parker, L. H., Rennie, L. J., & Fraser, B. J. (Eds) (1996). *Gender, science and mathematics: Shortening the shadow*. Dordrecht, The Netherlands: Kluwer Academic Publishers.

INDEX